D1794462

Identity in the Age of the New Economy

Identity in the Age of the New Economy

Life in Temporary and Scattered Work Practices

Edited by

Torben Elgaard Jensen

Assistant Professor, Department of Organization and Industrial Sociology, Copenhagen Business School, Denmark

and

Ann Westenholz

Professor, Department of Organization and Industrial Sociology, Copenhagen Business School, Denmark

With an Afterword by

Paul du Gay

Professor of Sociology and Organization Studies in the Faculty of Social Sciences at the Open University, UK

Edward Elgar

Cheltenham, UK • Northampton, MA, USA

© Torben Elgaard Jensen and Ann Westenholz, 2004

All rights reserved. No part of this publication may be reproduced, stored in a retrieval system or transmitted in any form or by any means, electronic, mechanical or photocopying, recording, or otherwise without the prior permission of the publisher.

Published by
Edward Elgar Publishing Limited
Glensanda House
Montpellier Parade
Cheltenham
Glos GL50 1UA
UK

Edward Elgar Publishing, Inc.
136 West Street
Suite 202
Northampton
Massachusetts 01060
USA

A catalogue record for this book
is available from the British Library

ISBN 1 84376 639 6

Printed and bound in Great Britain by MPG Books Ltd, Bodmin, Cornwall

Contents

List of figures and tables	vi
List of contributors	vii
Acknowledgements	x

Introduction: studies of work and identity beyond the epochal *Torben Elgaard Jensen and Ann Westenholz*	1
1 The culturalization of work in the 'new' economy: an historical view *Liz McFall*	9
2 Changing times, changing identities: a case study of British journalists *Gill Ursell*	34
3 The networking arena *Torben Elgaard Jensen*	55
4 Temporary stars – the rise and fall of a talent agency *Lars Strannegård and Ola Bergström*	79
5 On becoming a freelance creative professional *Ellen Van Wijk and Peter Leisink*	99
6 Emerging identities beyond organizational boundaries *Ann Westenholz*	122
Afterword: the tyranny of the epochal and work identity *Paul du Gay*	147
Index	159

Figures and tables

FIGURES

0.1	Location of the book in the theoretical landscape	7
3.1	Analytical model	64
4.1	Execency's presentation to investors, talents and customers	92
6.1	Three emerging identities in work practice	139

TABLES

3.1	Three versions of network	62
6.1	Dimensions in four field identity stories	131

Contributors

Ola Bergström is Assistant Professor at the Gothenburg School of Economics and Commercial Law at Göteborg University. He received his PhD with a study of recruitment management. He has been a visiting scholar at the Scandinavian Centre for Organization Research at Stanford University. His current research focuses on the interface between organizations and the labour market. He has worked extensively with a number of EU projects and has published books and articles on recruitment and contingent work in Europe and the United States.

Paul du Gay is Professor of Sociology and Organization Studies, and Co-Director of the Centre for Citizenship, Identity and Governance, in the Faculty of Social Sciences at the Open University, UK. His recent published work includes *In Praise of Bureaucracy* (Sage, 2000) and *Cultural Economy* (edited with Mike Pryke, Sage, 2002). He is currently working on a book for Sage provisionally entitled *Culture, Person and Organization* and also undertaking a cultural and historical analysis of the development of self-service retailing in Britain.

Torben Elgaard Jensen is Assistant Professor at the Department of Organization and Industrial Sociology, Copenhagen Business School, Denmark. He received his PhD with a study of the reorganization of social work in the municipality of Copenhagen. His current research interest is in the sociology of work, in particular the materialities of organizing and the potential effectiveness of temporary arrangements of work and identities. He is currently working on the research project 'Relational Identities in Temporary and Scattered Work Practice'.

Peter Leisink is Professor of Public Management and Organization Studies at the Utrecht School of Governance, Utrecht University, The Netherlands. He (co-)edited several publications including *Work and Citizenship in the New Europe* (Edward Elgar, 1993), *The Challenges to Trade Unions in Europe* (Edward Elgar, 1996), *Globalization and Labour Relations* (Edward Elgar, 1999) and *Organizational Relationships in the Networking Age* (Edward Elgar, 2003).

Liz McFall is a lecturer in sociology at the Open University, UK. She has published a number of articles and a book *Advertising: A Cultural Economy* (Sage, 2004) exploring the cultural economy of advertising practice from an historical perspective. Her current research interests include work in the new economy and the historical formation of markets for life insurance.

Lars Strannegård is an Associate Professor at the Centre for Advanced Studies in Leadership at the Stockholm School of Economics. He received his PhD with a study of change management and leadership in the global appliance manufacturer Electrolux. He has been a visiting scholar at the University of St Gallen in Switzerland and at the Scandinavian Centre for Organization Research at Stanford University, USA. His current research focuses on leadership and technology, the dynamics of projects that fail, and issues of brand management. He has published books and articles on branding, the relationship between organization and technology and change management.

Gill Ursell was the originator of specialized journalism tuition at Trinity and All Saints, University of Leeds, UK, introducing journalism studies to the undergraduate programme in the early 1980s and vocationally oriented diplomas in 1989. She is a council member of the Broadcast Journalism Training Council, UK and also participates in the regional centres of the National Council for the Training of Journalists and the Royal Television Society, UK. Academically, her work builds upon a substantial history of empirically grounded analyses of work organization and employment relations. In 1992, this involved an investigation of work and employment change in British television, for which, in 1997, she was awarded her doctorate. Her most recent publications are 'Dumbing Down or Shaping Up? New technologies, new media, new journalism', *Journalism: Theory, Practice and Criticism*, 2001, **2** (2), 175–96 and 'Creating Value and Valuing Creation in Contemporary UK Television: or "dumbing down" the workforce', *Journalism Studies*, 2003, **4** (1), 31–46.

Ellen Van Wijk teaches in Public Management and Organization Studies at the Utrecht School of Governance, Utrecht University, The Netherlands. She is also a PhD student at CERES Research School, The Netherlands, where she preparing a thesis on 'Identity Construction and Commitments in Organizations'. A recent chapter on 'Identity Construction and Commitments of Graphic Designers' appeared in W. Koot, P. Leisink and P. Verweel (eds), *Organizational Relationships in the Networking Age* (Edward Elgar, 2003).

Ann Westenholz is Professor of Management and Strategy at the Department of Organization and Industrial Sociology, Copenhagen Business School, Denmark. She is currently the leader of a research project about 'Relational Identities in Temporary and Scattered Work Practice' financed by the Danish Social Science Research Council. Her long-standing research interest is in workplace democracy and among her latest publications is 'Organizational Citizens – Unionized Wage Earners, Participative Management, and Beyond' in *The Northern Lights – Organization Theory in Scandinavia*, edited by Barbara Czarniawska and Guje Sevón (Copenhagen Business School Press, 2003).

Acknowledgements

We thank the Danish Social Science Research Council and the Danish Society for the Advancement of Business Education for their financial support for the process which has resulted in the present book. We also wish to thank the publisher's anonymous referees, from whom we have drawn inspiration in completing the contributions, and especially Paul du Gay, with whom we have discussed most of the chapters. Marianne Risberg, of the Department of Organization and Industrial Sociology, Copenhagen Business School, has been of invaluable assistance in preparing the final layout of the book.

Torben Elgaard Jensen and Ann Westenholz

Introduction: studies of work and identity beyond the epochal

Torben Elgaard Jensen and Ann Westenholz

The nexus between identity and the organization of work life has been explored in a diverse array of social science traditions, from Weber's link between bureaucracies and protestant ethics to Giddens's link between disembedded, globalized institutions and self-reflexive identities.

In the past decade, there has been a sharp increase in a particular kind of story about identity and work life. The story, told with increasing frequency, suggests that there has been a rupture with a more stable past; work life has changed quite dramatically, and the consequences for identity are only beginning to dawn on us. The story comes in various versions:

- It is argued that careers are becoming boundaryless as opposed to the bounded careers of earlier times.
- It is argued that lifelong employment will be replaced by ever more short-term employment, contracting, and freelancing.
- It is argued that working is increasingly about individual networking as opposed to the formalized and bureaucratic work organization of yesterday.
- It is argued that a pervasive scattering of communities is taking place as opposed to the more coherent and consistent communities of the past.
- It is argued that a new economy is superseding an old economy.
- In general, it is argued that organizations are becoming much more flexible and thus demanding much more flexibility of their members.

What then, does this supposed rupture mean to identity? The disagreement in the social science literature and the popular press is considerable. On the one hand, a number of authors suggest that nothing less than a social disaster is developing. In the past, the labour market was characterized by a relatively large core of stable employment. This middle class haven was surrounded by a periphery, a secondary labour market with unattractive working conditions: more tedious jobs, lower wages, less education, poorer promotion possibilities, and primarily lower job security. What is happening at present is the flooding of the core by the conditions of the periphery. Working people in all segments of the labour market are forced to change jobs, future plans, colleagues and location much more frequently. Insecurity is thus spreading everywhere. This development, it is argued, has profound consequences at a social psychological level. Constant changes and the impossibility of long-term planning lead to disorientation and, in the words of Richard Sennett, the corrosion of character.

There are others authors, however, who take a completely opposite view on identity and recent changes in work life. They argue that we are currently witnessing the emergence of a new heroic figure in the labour market, which they call 'free agents'. These are typically highly skilled professionals, who sell their expertise to the highest bidder. This élite workforce migrates from business to business and reaps the benefits of flexibility, variation and extremely high salaries. The increased flexibility of the labour markets thus enhances rather than undermines the possibilities for human self-actualization. The creativity, responsibility and energy of the individual is finally being liberated from the embrace of too big and too bureaucratic organizations.

Which of the two suggested trends should we believe? Will people become corroded characters or free agents? Will they break down or will they break free? Rather than siding with the pessimists or the optimists, the authors of the present volume dispute the basic premise of this polarized debate. We challenge the idea that a rupture has taken place, and that the development of work life can be adequately conceptualized as the spectacular shift from one epoch to the next. More specifically, we challenge the kinds of stories – epochalist stories – that dramatize present changes by making a contrast to a stable past.

A brief reflection on the history of work organization makes it plain that epochalist stories do not hold up to a closer scrutiny. First of all, the notion of work as a stable job within a stable organization seems to draw mainly on the particular bureaucratic organization of work, which became widespread after World War II in most western countries. However, this organisation of work hardly became an all-encompassing order.

If one goes further back in history, it is obvious that 'stable jobs in stable organizations' become an even more problematic shorthand for 'work in the past'. One merely has to mention the 'boundaryless careers' of travelling journeymen, the 'project organizations' of theatre companies, or the 'networking environments' of medieval markets, to make clear that the so-called new forms of work have been around for quite a long time.

For this reason, the study of contemporary identity and various non-bureaucratic forms of work should not seek justification by pitching itself against a spurious assumption about a stable and well-ordered past. Quite the opposite: the relevance of this area of study is precisely that work has been done and identities constructed in this way for a very long time. What is important then, is to tell stories of the current transformation of work and identities that recognize the heterogeneity of work life and that build a theoretical agenda beyond grand-scale epochalist claims.

In order to make a collective contribution to this project, the authors of the present volume have made certain theoretical choices. The first has already been mentioned. It is the enabling negative of not doing epochalist explanations. However, since epochalist stories are very much a part of present social science debates, it would be unproductive simply to ignore them. For this reason, each author addresses a specific epochalist assumption, which is then challenged and complexified by means of a thorough empirical analysis. The authors frame their analyses and develop their arguments along particular lines, which we will briefly sketch out.

The first, and perhaps most obvious way to challenge epochalist assumptions, is to do a historical analysis. Does the projected image of the past really hold up to closer scrutiny if one digs into the archives? This type of analysis often results in surprisingly rich and complex accounts, which not only challenge epochalist simplifications but also makes one wonder how these simplifications became so convincing in the first place. Unfortunately, historical analysis is sadly underrepresented in the contemporary academic world, which seems obsessed with present events.

The second approach of the authors of this volume is to explore contemporary work and identities in ethnographic detail. Through these accounts and this form of analysis, the authors develop empirically grounded discussion of epochalist claims. How are the putative great shifts performed in practice? What specifically do people say about recent changes? Does the new really displace the old, or is the empirical reality better described as complex patterns of interference?

The third approach is to make epochalism itself an object of study. Epochalism is not merely a feature of the talk and texts of professional theoreticians. It is just as much a part of the daily discursive practice of working life. By studying epochalist discourse in action, it is possible not only to make an interesting account of practice, but also to deconstruct the universalistic claims that epochs are simply the way things are. Rather, epochs are the way things get constructed in particular moments at particular locations by particular actors.

A fourth approach, which overlaps with several of the above mentioned, might be labelled the critical case approach. Epochalist accounts often trade on stories of particular professions or segments of the labour market (for example cultural intermediaries) that signify the advent of a New World. This makes a closer investigation of these cases particularly interesting in order to evaluate these claims and search for possible alternative interpretations.

In sum, one may characterize the analytical stance of the book in the following way. The authors are scaling down in the sense that they refrain from making sweeping, broad scale claims about the new world order of work. But at the same time, they are scaling up in the sense that they increase the amount and the quality of the data used to discuss particular developments in work and identity.

The challenge of epochalism is the first theoretical choice that informs the authors. The second is the focus on identity, or to be more precise, relational identity. The authors partake in the broad constructionist movement, which takes identity to be an emerging effect of on-going relations rather than an internal, pre-given essence. The construction of identity is a matter of making, distinguishing or identifying people in a field of relationships. The emergence of relational identity depends on immediate interaction with people and physical surroundings. But relationality also includes mediated interaction that stretches far beyond the current situation in time and space. Talking about relational identity is thus a rather open agenda, which makes it possible to explore the construction of identity through a wealth of empirical materials.

Where on earth would one expect to find the dramatic effects announced by epochalist commentators? Where in the economy? And in which segments of the workforce? Although the answers to these questions vary to some degree, the general belief seems to be that highly innovative endeavours and 'the economy' are driven by the western world, the private sector, and the highly-skilled segments of the workforce. These assumptions may be questioned or criticized, but if one wants to argue with epochalist accounts, it is nevertheless productive to direct the focus toward the same empirical field. This is what the authors of the present book do: all cases are in the private sector, all cases are located in Western Europe or North America and all cases relate to the higher-skilled segments of the workforce. Within this shared focus, however, a broad variety is covered. The topics include technical work, creative work, communicative work and managerial work. The degree of institutionalization differs considerably: on the one hand there are studies of old and well-established fields such as journalism, graphic design and advertising. On the other hand there are analyses of relatively new or relatively ill-defined areas, such as software development or the work of starting up a 'new economy' firm. In addition, the cases cover almost the entire spectrum of employment relations: the chapters are populated by company owners, middle managers, employees and consultants, as well as temporary workers.

The diversity of empirical material, even within the narrow overall frame, is an important part of the non-epochalist story. What is evidenced throughout the chapters is a striking variety in the development of (western, professional, private sector) work life. An assumption about a single all-encompassing developmental trend simply does not do justice to the empirical material. In combination, the chapters suggest a multi-faceted view of contemporary work that questions a number of the epochalist myths related to the so-called new economy, knowledge society or network society. In the next section, we shall briefly introduce the chapters.

In the first chapter, Liz McFall challenges the notion that the 'new' economy is distinct from the 'old' economy because it is based on non-standard manipulation of symbolic or cultural knowledge and information. The proponents of the thesis of 'culturalization of work' have described the appearance of new categories of worker such as 'symbolic analysts' and 'cultural intermediaries' that perform this 'new' blending of culture and work. Furthermore, these authors have argued that the culturalization of work entails the demise of work-based identity and the advent of identity based on consumption. McFall questions this entire line of reasoning by investigating the root assumption that work in the past was separated from culture. Through empirical examples of historical advertising practices and theoretical analysis, McFall argues that work is necessarily culturally constituted. In this way she argues against the notion of a major shift and for a more multifaceted view of identity.

Gill Ursell also challenges the assumption that 'cultural intermediaries' represent a new and victorious type of worker in a transformed labour market. Ursell traces the development of journalistic work through a historical analysis of public ideals of journalism, media ownership, work organization and career patterns. Rather than the persistence of a creative and independent ideal, Ursell's account reveals the serious undermining of traditional ideals of public journalism. The analysis of journalism is an interesting counter-story to the prevalent claim that 'cultural intermediaries' represent the most innovative and flourishing part of the labour market. On the contrary, Ursell suggests that a remarkable standardization and trivialization has taken place.

Torben Elgaard Jensen investigates the idea of networking, which is a recurrent element in epochalist accounts of the labour market. In many of these accounts, networking is depicted as the novel organizational principle of connecting everything with everything. Elgaard Jensen, however, questions this idea through an ethnographic study of a particular network environment, an office hotel for small innovative firms. In this location, the term networking seems to cover a number of different and to some extent irreconcilable organizing efforts. It is simultaneously the construction of an exclusive club, the establishment of formalized relations between buyers and sellers, and the generation of a loose assemblage of acquaintances. Elgaard Jensen explores the conflicts and synergies between these different versions of networking, and he argues that this tensioned pattern forms particular conditions of possibility for the construction of identity.

Ola Bergström and Lars Strannegård examine the practical workings of the epochalist discourse through a case study of the rise and fall of a talent agency. The agency draws heavily on epochalist ideas and rhetoric in the construction of claims about its unique identity as a company. It argues that there is a gap between the old and the new economy, and that the talent agency is able to bridge this gap for a number of actors. Investors will want to place their money in a new economy firm such as the talent agency. Clients will need the talent agency to recruit the business talent that will transform companies and help them survive in the new situation. Talents will need the agency to maximize their market value. By following the company and its epochalist discourse from the beginning to the end, Bergström and Strannegård examine the stability and vulnerability of this particular construction of organizational identity.

In creative professions, the 'need' to express creativity and individuality is often quoted as the reason for becoming self-employed. In Ellen van Wijk and Peter Leisink's study of graphic designers, the construction and workings of this need are explored, from the ideals conveyed at Art College through the narratives of employed designers, to the accounts given by designers who have recently started on their own. Van Wijk and Leisink's analysis demonstrates that independence seems to be a normative and conversational ideal, which is adhered to despite fulfilling working conditions as an employee, and despite obstacles related to self-employment. It suggests that the yearning for independence might be better explained by long-standing professional ideals than by recent economic pressures.

Ann Westenholz scrutinizes the relation between identity and organizational boundaries in her study of IT professionals. She identifies four identity stories which are widely known and available in the IT field. One of these stories, 'the citizen in the company', depends on a clearly bounded organization, whereas other stories – 'the open-source grassrooter', 'the free agent in the market', and 'the project maker in professional communities' – do not. Through her analysis of specific negotiations of meaning and identity, Westenholz demonstrates how a number of extra-organizational narrative forms are employed, combined and developed in the situated construction of identity. The assumption that a recognizable identity by necessity depends on organizational boundaries is thus rejected.

In the afterword Paul du Gay reflects on the previous chapters and the issues of organizational change, work identity and the 'tyranny of the epochal'.

In this final part of the introduction, we would like to indicate our ideas about the location of the present book in a broader theoretical landscape. This book, we believe, is related to a number of well-established academic fields, such as Identity Studies, Human Resource Management, Industrial Relations and Organizational Studies. But the approach differs from the mainstreams of these traditions, and partakes in recent developments within these. In Figure

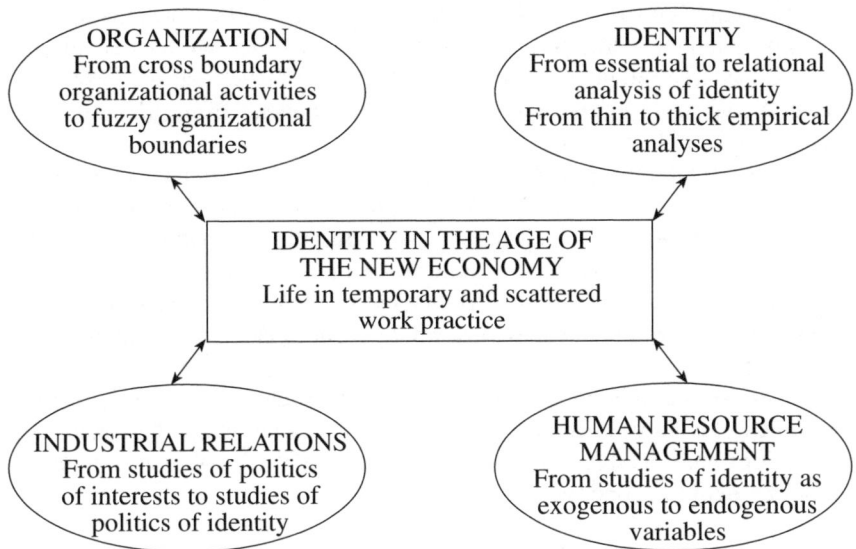

Figure 0.1   Location of the book in the theoretical landscape

0.1 and the next section, mainstream and recent developments are described.

The essentialist perspective on the individual, which is well known from psychology, characterizes a major part of identity studies. *Identity in the Age of the New Economy* deviates from the essentialist perspective and follows the path of recent years' sociological/social-psychological analyses of identities. The latter analyses evoke a relational perspective, and have been predominantly theoretical in addressing the situation of the individual in contemporary society. In contrast, the present book presents thick empirical studies of relational identities in scattered and temporary work practices.

Within Human Resource Management, identities are often seen as exogenous variables and analyses tend to be governed by managerial perspectives. In that context the contingent labour force is often characterized as disloyal. Based on empirical studies of temporary and scattered working life, this book demonstrates how identities are endogenous variables. Identity, for example loyalty/disloyalty toward the company and the work, is not something the individual 'is', but something that emerges through relations. The focus is thus directed away from the employment contract as being decisive for loyalty and toward studies of relational situations in diverse types of practice (work practice, education, and so on).

Many scholars within the tradition of Industrial Relations are deeply engaged in studying the growth in contingent labour – especially in low-skilled labour. The assumption is that contingent labour is driven away from the primary labour market into a secondary one, and that the interests of this group are poorly safeguarded. In this context, the book focuses on highly-educated contingent employees and directs the analyses from the politics of interests to the politics of identities.

Mainstream Organization Theory assumes organizations to have boundaries delimiting the internal from the external. In recent years, there has been a growing interest in studies focusing on actors crossing the boundaries between internal and external. This book aims to demonstrate that boundaries are emerging concurrently with the development of identities: there is a concern with fuzzy organizational boundaries, which is not found in most organization studies.

We believe that this book will be of interest to scholars within these four academic fields. It is aimed primarily at people working within the disciplines of sociology and social psychology, although it will also be of interest to those within the field of economics.

1. The culturalization of work in the 'new' economy: an historical view

Liz McFall

INTRODUCTION

> *Each* of us is aware, emotionally and intellectually, that we are potentially unemployed, potentially underemployed, potentially insecure or temporary workers, potential 'part-timers'. ... the central figure of our society – and the 'normal' condition within that society – is no longer (or is tending no longer to be) that of the 'worker'. It is becoming rather the figure of the insecure worker ... (Gorz 1999, p. 53)

Gorz's measured summation of what is happening to work and working identities in the 'new' – that is to say, knowledge- or information-based – economy, resonates with much that has been written on the subject. The scenarios that different authors describe range from the wildly optimistic to the cataclysmically bleak, deploying styles and evidence ranging from apocalyptic hyperbole to dense, statistically informed projection. Perhaps the only point on which there is widespread agreement is that substantive restructuring of the economy at a global level is underway, occasioned by an increasing dependence on knowledge or information resources; and that this will, in fact has already begun to, irretrievably transform the character of work. The scale and scope of economic restructuring mean that its effects are to be felt not just upon employment and work but on the entire 'social landscape of human life' (Castells 2000, p. 1). This transformation is too profound to put down to simple historical change; rather, a sense of a complete break or rupture with the past pervades much of the literature in references to both endings, new ages and new beginnings (for example Rifkin 1995; Castells 2000; Beck 2000). A new epoch, in which no aspect of social life will be quite as it was, is thought to be upon us. If the character of economy, production and work is to be permanently transfigured, this is to be matched by equally tenacious changes in culture, consumption and leisure.

At their best, such accounts marshal an impressive wealth of evidence in justification of their ambition, but they nevertheless remain reliant on the device of simple opposition. What is distinctive about 'now' emerges through being held up against a simpler, slower, more settled and more solid past. The contemporary characterization of the economy as driven by fast and fragile networks, information, knowledge and symbolic exchange invokes a past of fixed and enduring ties and tangible, material exchange. But past/present is not the only dualism at work in accounts of the information/knowledge society – an equally powerful opposition is deployed in the characterization of economy and culture. Economy, closely associated with production and work, is understood as properly separate, sealed off and distinct from the fields of culture, consumption and leisure. In some accounts of the emerging epoch, this normative separation has itself been compromised by global economic restructuring. The aim in this chapter is, first of all, to trace the influence of both past/present and economy/culture oppositions in a brief review of accounts of the transformation of work in the information/knowledge society. Such accounts vary enormously, but whether the emphasis is on the demise of work-based identities, the triumph of commoditized culture or the unprecedented pre-eminence of intellectual capital, questions of culture and 'culturalization' figure prominently. Contemporary advertising, poised between production and consumption and charged with endowing symbolic appeal to material goods, is often invoked as an ideal exemplar of the culturalization of economic practice. Yet scant attention has been paid to the historically precedented nature of its role in this regard. The second part of the chapter aims to show through a review of empirical evidence that working practices in advertising were historically culturally constituted – not primarily because they aimed to endow the material with symbolic value, but because economic practices are simultaneously and inescapably cultural practices.

THE CULTURALIZATION OF WORK?

In the last decades of the twentieth century, one conceptual challenge seemed to gain precedence over all others in social theory. That challenge came in the form of what Turner (1992) has called the 'caesural' impulse to define the character of the break between an historical epoch that was widely understood to be ending and one that had recently begun. This resulted in a bewildering display of intellectual diagnostics in which the epochal condition was to be captured by terms like post-industrial, post-Fordist, post-modern, consumer, information, risk or knowledge. These terms frequently overlapped, often representing different perspectives on similar substantive changes, in particular in the global organization of production, the pace of technological change, the significance of information or knowledge-based resources, the character of consumption and finally the consequences to human subjectivity, identity or reflexivity of the shifting dynamics between all of the above. While there is not the space here to do anything like justice to this vast literature, the aim in this section is nevertheless to pull out some recurring themes in regard to the transformation of work. In particular, attention focuses on how the shift to an information- or knowledge-based economy is thought to have impacted upon work and identities and their relation to culture and consumption.

Contemporary concerns about the fate of work in a 'post' industrial, information-based epoch have an intellectual lineage stretching at least as far back as the 1970s (Bell 1973; Toffler 1970; Touraine 1974). Such concerns have been given renewed impetus in more recent work by authors like Beck (2000), Castells (2000), Gorz (1999), Lash and Urry (1987, 1994) and Sennett (1998). What unites this diverse body of literature is a preoccupation with the profound transformations wrought across all domains of social life by the restructuring of the global capitalist economy. In his encyclopaedic three volume treatise on the information age, Castells (2000, 1997, 1998) defines its basis not in information, technology or knowledge *per se* but in what he terms informationalism. The historical distinctiveness of informationalism rests on the realization of the productivity potential inherent in the development of a technological paradigm based in information technology. This involves a generalization of information- and knowledge-based production across the entire field of global economic processes and necessitates not only economic, but social, cultural and institutional transformations.

> This is why the economy is informational, not just information-based, because the cultural-institutional attributes of the whole social system must be included in the diffusion and implementation of the new technological paradigm, as the industrial economy was not merely based on the use of new sources of energy for manufacturing but on the emergence of an industrial culture, characterized by a new social and technical division of labour. (Castells 2000, p. 100)

The advent of informationalism, then, facilitated by new information technologies and spurred on by global competition, has resulted in the restructuring of firms and organizations and is thus bound to usher in a whole host of transformations to the content, organization, conditions and character of work. The most fundamental of these transformations is what Castells terms the 'individualization of labor in the labor process' (2000, p. 282).

Individualization reverses the historical trends of the industrial era towards mass production, salarization and the socialization of the work process and produces instead customized markets, decentralized management, individualized work and segmented work processes. Information technologies permit the organizational and spatial decentralization of work tasks and their coordination in real time as evidenced in the growth of business practices like outsourcing, subcontracting, consulting and downsizing. The 'standard pattern of employment' with its emphasis on fixed working hours, job stability, fixed and agreed location of work and a social contract between employer and employee has given way to 'flexible' working patterns. As its name suggests, flexible work is characterized by more fluid and negotiable definitions of work time and location, by task-oriented contracts with no commitment to future job stability and a much diminished social contract. Notwithstanding the gravity of such changes, Castells resists the baleful scenarios painted by some authors prophesying the 'end of work'. Rather, he argues 'there are more jobs and a higher proportion of people employed than at any time in history. ... the diffusion of information technologies, while certainly displacing some workers and eliminating some jobs, has not resulted and it does not seem that it will result in the foreseeable future, in mass unemployment' (2000, p. 505).

Castells is similarly unimpressed by the widely circulating narratives regarding the polarization of work in the information/knowledge economy. At the simplest level, this view, of which there are many variants, forecasts a divergence in the fortunes of a small élite group of knowledge workers and information analysts – the winners – and a much larger group of deskilled and underemployed labour – the losers (see for example Beck 2000; Gorz 1999; Rifkin 1995; Ritzer 1998; Sennett 1998). Castells concludes that the popular image of the informational economy as one characterized by a technologically driven, disproportionate growth of low-level service jobs or 'McJobs' against a slower growth in professional or technical jobs is not borne out by the evidence he amassed. This, however, does not amount to an argument that the informational society is one where polarization and inequality do not feature. Rather, it is an argument about what the nature and sources of such polarization are. In Castells's view it is not information technology or occupational differentiation in themselves that produce inequality, but differential social and managerial practices across sectors, firms and territories and their interaction with gender, ethnicity and age characteristics.

> The resulting bifurcation of work patterns and polarization of labour is not the necessary result of technological progress or of inexorable evolutionary trends (for example, the rise of the 'post-industrial society' or the 'service economy'). It is socially determined and managerially designed in the process of the capitalist restructuring taking place at the shop floor level, within the framework and with the help of the process of technological change at the roots of the informational paradigm. (2000, pp. 266–7)

Castels's account is distinguished by the density of evidence and analysis he presents and by the careful moderation of many of the claims he makes. Yet despite his insistence that the informational society is neither technologically given nor the inevitable result of a predetermined historical evolution, the entire dynamic of the book leads nevertheless in this direction. To this extent his account functions to temper, but not contradict, the epochal impulse in social theory.

This impulse often manifests itself in accounts of an irresistible transformation of the character and place of work and thereby identities, in restructured economies. Work is understood to be subject to a range of processes including deskilling, casualization, individualization, flexibilization and feminization, with the result that the insecure, temporary and flexible worker dominates in a society no longer rooted in the rhythms of paid, fulltime work.[1] In Beck's account, the transition currently underway is to a 'second modernity' of reflexive modernization, a term he uses to signal a shift 'away from a first modernity locked within the national state, and towards a second, open, risk-filled modernity characterized by general insecurity' (2000, p. 19). The second modernity is defined by the predominance of science-based information technologies, globalization, ecological crises and individualization, and each of these carries potential negative and positive consequences for the future of work. These consequences, however, allow the possibility for a redefinition of work such that the full employment framework becomes superseded by a 'multi-activity society' (2000, p. 36) in which the idea of work as the only possible foundation for identity is finally abandoned. Instead the multi-activity society is characterized by individualized life patterns and 'civil labour', a form of 'voluntary, self-organized labour, where what should be done, and how it should be done are in the hands of those who actually do it' (2000, p. 127). Civil labour takes the place of paid work as the key determinant of identity in the second modernity.

Beck's model of a new individualized mode of civic behaviour seems intended more as a polemical intervention than a description of observable conditions, but his emphasis on the demise of a work-based society is a familiar theme in epochal accounts. Few may regard this as a literal 'end of work' in Rifkin's (1995) sense, but the idea that work will no longer function as the primary structure of social life has considerable currency. If work is now more fragile, temporary and insecure, so the argument goes, it is consequently a less reliable basis on which to pin identity or what Sennett (1998) calls 'character'. Under such conditions the 'work ethic' begins to lose its purchase.

> The work ethic is the arena in which the depth of experience is most challenged today. The work ethic, as we commonly understand it, asserts disciplined use of one's time and the value of delayed gratification. ... [People] worked hard and they waited, this was their psychological experience of depth. Such a work ethic depends in part on institutions stable enough for a person to practice delay. Delayed gratification loses its value though in a regime whose institutions change rapidly ... (Sennett, 1998, pp. 98–9)

Under rapidly changing conditions, work and production recede as the primary grounds on which individual identities are negotiated, to be replaced by culture and consumption (Sennett 2001; Smart 2003). This shift in the basis of identity is, in many accounts, an inevitable corollary of the broader shift to a 'consumer', or 'postmodern' society (Bauman 1998). In a society where 'identities are now rarely built to last, and increasingly lack the foundation of a permanent job, secure work or a career' (Smart 2003, p. 74) consumption emerges as the ideal means through which to construct identities. For Bauman (1998, p. 24), where once individuals engaged with society primarily in their capacity as producers, in 'late-modern, second modern or post-modern' times, social engagement is primarily as consumers. It is non-work life, the activities, practices and routines of leisure and consumption through which individuals increasingly find meaning and a basis for identity (Gorz 1999; Smart 2003). Where consumption was once understood as a pacifying compensation for the rigours and deprivations imposed by the demands of paid work, it now becomes the primary motivation for work (Gorz 1999). The aesthetics of consumption thus triumph over work as the basis of identity. Such identities, however, are built from fragile and transitory 'cultural' meanings circulating in the market and are held in sharp contrast to the more solid stuff of identities grafted from the economic structures of work and production.

The emergence of consumption-based identities corresponds to broader shifts in the character of consumption. Under contemporary conditions, consumption is not based on materially defined 'needs' or on the desire for social distinction. It is, in Bauman's terms, emancipated from 'its past instrumentality' and absolved 'from the need to justify itself by reference to anything but its own pleasurability' (2001, pp. 12–13). Bauman draws on Baudrillard's (1988) account of a consumer society structured by the symbolic exchange of sign value. Drawing on insights from semiotics, Baudrillard argued that the 'use value' of objects has been subordinated to 'exchange value' under the auspices of the 'commodity-sign'. Commodity-signs are consumed for their cultural meanings in contemporary society, not for their material characteristics. Through the symbolic exchange of commodity-sign values, consumption is able to meet a need – opened up by the decline of social institutions and traditions – for difference and social meaning. In Lash and Urry's (1994) account, this shift in the character of consumption is symptomatic of a broader process of individualization, which releases consumption from the dictates of family, corporate group and social class. Thus 'whole areas of lifestyle and consumer choice are freed up and individuals are forced to decide, to take risks, to bear responsibilities, to be actively involved in the construction of their own identities for themselves' (1994, p. 61).

This sea change in the role of consumption is central to many accounts of the post-industrial, information/knowledge society and is attributed, at least in part, to the apparatus of advertising and marketing (Beck, Giddens and Lash 1994; Featherstone 1991; Lash and Urry 1994). The unprecedented pre-eminence of advertising, for some theorists, is thought to have a pollutant effect on 'culture', making it increasingly difficult to differentiate between culture, commerce and branding (Mattelart 1991; Wernick 1991). By merging economic objectives with cultural knowledge, advertising plays a significant role in what Lash and Urry (1994) describe as the shift in reflexive modernity to economic growth grounded in 'reflexive accumulation'. This term is meant to signal the contemporary blurring of the processes of (economic) accumulation and (cultural) reflexivity such that the two are 'more than ever interlaced and interarticulated' (1994, p. 64). Indeed for Lash and Urry, the information/knowledge society is 'culture laden' – based around information/knowledge processing capacities which are themselves, cultural.

> This is more than an aestheticization of everyday life. It is a *Vergesellschaftung* (societalization) of culture, rather similar to an earlier societalization of the industrial principle. The societalization of culture is the principle even of an ever more information-intensive industrial production. That is, though manufacturing decidedly matters, it is itself increasingly information-(hence culture-) intensive. (1994, p. 143)

It is clear that whether judged as 'contamination' or 'interarticulation', the de-differentiation of the cultural and the economic is a peculiar state of affairs. Whatever differences persist between the various accounts of work in the emerging epoch, work properly belongs in the sphere of production and the economic and this is held to be quite apart from consumption and the cultural. The cultural is theorized as normatively 'outside' of production and the economic, as in Castells's remark that the transformations associated with the network society 'go beyond the sphere of social and technical relationships of production: they deeply affect culture and power *as well*' (2000, p. 507, my emphasis). Even Lash and Urry's model of a hybrid mode of 'reflexive accumulation' presupposes a prior history in which culture and economy were more clearly differentiated.

This type of thinking is undoubtedly convenient from an analytical viewpoint – it is much easier to think about social life if these categories are kept separate. But however compelling in abstract terms, dividing cultural and economic activity in material practice is quite a different matter. Where culture is defined in Hall's (1997) sense as that concerning human meanings and values, it becomes clear that an economic domain apart from culture is almost impossible to conceptualize. Whether this interarticulation is best understood as a generalized characteristic or as a specific product of an epochal implosion has been the subject of some recent scrutiny. Ray and

Sayer's (1999) discussion, for instance, identifies the dependence of contemporary accounts of the 'de-differentiation' of culture and economy on a general distinction between 'cultural' and 'economic' logics, which they concede is difficult to sustain. Nevertheless, they see the continued deployment of culture and economy as separate terms as evidence that their distinction remains politically and theoretically important. They argue therefore that, however awkward, a distinction should be maintained between an economic logic based on the external, instrumental calculation of means/ends relations and a cultural logic based on intrinsically meaningful activities, artefacts and relationships. This sort of distinction depends on a conceptual separation of instrumental and intrinsic value, that however convincing in the abstract, is extraordinarily difficult to apply in practice.

As du Gay and Pryke's (2002, pp. 8–12) contribution to the debate has it, instrumental, economic action is not only the product of socio-cultural relations of training and practice within specific contexts, but itself gives rise to substantive, cultural goals. There is then no single, unified 'cultural' logic but an array of cultural interests and capacities that are the plural creation of particular historically-specific religious, legal, aesthetic, economic and educational regimes. For this reason, 'any attempt to instigate categorical distinctions between 'intrinsically' and 'instrumentally' oriented activity in order to support a general normative analysis of economic and cultural life will quickly come up against brute empirical realities that it will not be able to account for or make much reasonable sense of' (du Gay and Pryke 2002, p. 11). This has strong parallels with recent work in the anthropology of science and techniques (AST) (Callon 1998; Callon *et al.* 2002; Law 2002). The domains of culture and economy are understood in this critical trajectory not as ahistorical realities but as the results of specific processes of configuration. Culture, according to Law, is everywhere including in what he terms 'economically relevant activity' and there is nothing new in this.

> [I]f we are to talk about culture at all, then it certainly doesn't exist in the abstract. It doesn't even simply exist as a set of discourses programmed into the body – although bodies are to be sure, crucial in the performances of culture. Instead ... culture is located and performed in human and non-human material practices. And these are material practices which extend beyond and implicate not only human beings, subjects and their meanings but also technical, architectural, geographical and corporeal arrangements. (2002, p. 24)

Law's approach involves recognizing that material practices are constituted by both cultural and economic elements that constantly interfere with each other. For Law, as for Callon (1998, 2002), the practices, subjects and cultures of economically relevant activity are 'performed' and thus always multiple, variable and incomplete. This emphasis on the performance of the economic may not be all that new – it certainly draws upon principles developed in structuralist and Foucauldian thought and elaborated in relation to economic life elsewhere[2] – but it offers a distinctive framework for analysing the material operation of given economic practices.

This theoretical perspective informs the approach taken to the empirical research described in the remainder of the chapter. The research comes in the form of an account of historical advertising practices. Historical advertising offers a particularly apt perspective to review recent debates about the transformation of work for a number of reasons. As signalled at the outset, such debates are frequently marked by a tendency to interpret substantive changes as evidence of the arrival of a new age or epoch. The present is thus understood as an era of sweeping changes in the global economy, fuelled by the acceleration of technological development, the expansion of consumption and market principles and an increasing dependence on knowledge/ information or cultural resources. Yet, as Davis and Scase (2000) point out, each of the institutions, companies and sectors at the centre of such transformations has its own context and history. These contextual circumstances are specific to particular industries and have materially shaped their responses to broader global, technological changes. Despite this, little detailed empirical research has been conducted to explore the historical development of the cultural industries at the core of the information age.

Advertising, however, is not only an industry in which creative, information or knowledge capital plays a central role, it is also an industry which is widely understood to occupy a uniquely mediative position between production and consumption (Leiss, Kline and Jhally 1990) or between economy and culture (Lash and Urry, 1994). This mediative position places advertising at the centre of epochal transformations – if the key axis of society has shifted to consumption, culture or knowledge, this shift has been enabled, at least in part, by the persuasive and pervasive presence of advertising. Historical advertising thus offers an ideal platform to explore the interconnections between economy and culture in material working practices. If, rather than being neatly demarcated, economy and culture emerge in instances of historical practice as inherently intercalibrated, the logic of theorizing the character of the epoch in terms of a wholesale shift to a basis in consumption, culture or knowledge and a concomitant shift in the foundations of identity from work to consumption is called into question.

THE CONSTITUENT CHARACTER OF HISTORICAL ADVERTISING WORK

The aim in what follows is to attempt to uncover some of the ways in which economic and cultural dimensions of practice were enacted through specific, technical and organizational arrangements in the developing field of advertising. This involves an understanding of the cultural, not as something that intervenes in economic processes, but as constitutive of them. Implicit in this is a move away from the notion that the cultural and the economic can be clearly delineated. Clearly this presupposes a departure from an enlightenment-derived idea of culture as synonymous with aesthetic achievement. It also invokes a proposition that if culture is to be understood as coterminous with the broad realm of human meanings, values and practices, it cannot be easily distinguished from the economic. It is not as if the economic could be thought of or understood in any useful way without the mediation of meanings, values and practices. Understanding the economy requires the application of specific processes, tools and techniques of cultural representation to enable charting, measurement and calculation to be performed (Buck-Morss 1995; Miller and Rose 1990; Miller 2001). This sort of representational work involves a kind of generative abstraction through which economic elements are codified and accorded material significance. This is not just a matter of putting the economy into language or into culture but is bound up with the development of those practices of calculation that define the economic. Thus material working practices always necessarily comprise a mixed and interarticulated set of both cultural and economic elements.

The upshot of this is that it is well nigh impossible to extract the cultural from the economic in instances of working practice, and the approach advocated here is therefore to focus on the performance of advertising as a constituent material practice. This term is intended to signal that working practices can never be purely cultural or purely economic, but will inevitably involve both dimensions. It is used in an effort to escape from the fruitless endeavour of defining precisely the extent of the cultural and the economic, and the boundary between them. Thinking of advertising as a constituent material practice offers an alternative to the critical invocation of an idealized past in which economy, production and work were more clearly delineated from culture and consumption. It focuses attention instead on the ways in which both these dimensions of practice were enacted through specific technical and organizational arrangements, in the developing field of advertising, as even the most mundane of activities comprises devices in the 'performance' of 'culture' and 'economy'.

This section aims to explore the persistent entanglement of culture and economy through the mechanism of the historical development of the three functional specialisms in advertising other than creative work – account management, media planning and research. Account management involves managing the link to the client; the media department plans, places and buys space and time in the various media deployed in a campaign; whilst the research department provides research information on markets, products, and consumers. The concentration on these specialisms rather than what is usually termed the 'creative' work of art and copy production is calculated to try and reinforce the idea that cultural work is not just the work of aesthetics and representation but is really all work. These specialisms represent the general approach to the structural organization of work that persisted in many agencies by the 1930s–1940s and were a function of industry-wide moves to formalize and professionalize the conduct of advertising.[3]

The first difficulty in tracking the development of the functional specialisms concerns the dissimilarity of the formal organizational structure adopted by agencies at particular moments in their history. Account executives, for instance, were not always account executives and this change is not simply one of designation. In Norris's memoir of his working life at the agency Sell's, beginning in 1911, the four key senior personnel were described as Senior Clerks (Norris, HATa). Their positions were, in some respects, similar to contemporary account executives, but there were also substantial differences, as these clerks had a much broader role than client management. As Reginald Browne, the grandson of the founder of T.B. Browne, the UK's largest agency in 1900, remembers it:

> There was no Creative Department ... 'Copy' and the form of the advertisement should be made entirely the concern of the man in the agency who knew the Product and the Client best – namely the Contact Man as he was then called. In addition to his other responsibilities, the Contact Man had therefore to be 'Creative'. He had to be capable of determining the selling points of the product, conceiving the best method of presenting them in an attractive manner, and of himself finding headlines, writing the copy, and in most cases giving the Art Studio a rough idea of the layout. (Browne, c. 1975, pp. 4–5, HATa)

The use of contact men to produce copy was likely to have been pragmatic. Between 1870 and 1920, agencies had very different policies regarding their primary functions and although some agencies were involved in the production of advertisements at least as early as 1870, it took many other agencies much longer to undertake production formally as one of their services. As described in Charles Raymond's memoir of agency life in this period:

> Mr Daniel M Lord of Lord and Thomas, told me years afterwards, that when an advertiser first asked him if he would not write and fix up an advertisement for him, he was aghast, and rather resented the idea he should be asked to do the advertiser's work for him. (Raymond, 1923, pp. 9–10, JWTa)

The involvement of clerks, managers and contact men in the preparation of copy and layouts was a particular phase in the development of 'full service' agencies at a time when copy production was not widely regarded as a specialist occupation. It was a task that a variety of people – advertisers, newspaper journalists, freelance writers and agency staff – dabbled in. This appears to have been the case in a number of agencies with surviving records of the period. Ayer's historian, Ralph Hower, describes the appointment of their first copywriter around 1891, yet the agency had been preparing copy for clients since 1880 (Hower 1939, pp. 94, 317). Similarly James Walter Thompson (JWT) himself is credited with involvement in the preparation of famous advertising campaigns for Eastman Kodak, the Prudential and Cream of Wheat in the 1890s. In spite of this, he felt the core business of advertising was space buying, and he resented the increasing emphasis on planning, research and copy preparation in the early part of the twentieth century. It is unsurprising then that during his era the copy department in the New York office, at its height, consisted of only one writer and two artists (Raymond, 1923, JWTa). 'All-rounders' were the key to production in this period.

> When he joined JWT, Mr Kohl relates, the degree of specialisation was undreamed of. Key men in the organisation were 15–18 advertising allrounders. Known as solicitors, these men brought in the accounts, serviced them, wrote the copy, organised the artwork – even supervised production. (Kohl, Dawkins papers, JWTa)

The work of these all-rounders cannot be easily classified as solely 'cultural' or 'economic', but in practice blended together meanings, values and calculation. This emerges more explicitly in a close exploration of the everyday business practices of Henry Sell of the London-based agency Sell's. Sell's main concern in the bulk of his surviving correspondence appears to have been liaising with clients and finding new business. This aspect of agency business is deeply immersed in what Moeran (1996, pp. 48–9) describes as 'human chemistry'. The significance of this commerce in human relations in winning and maintaining business emerges quite clearly in Sell's correspondence. In one letter, John Maddocks, a contact who had been asked by Sell to help him win business from Bovril responds:

> I dare not say any more to Bovril people than I did or they will think I am getting a commission for doing so – If you get the Advertising it will be on account of what I said and advised Mr X (*indecipherable*). We had a long talk in which he made certain complaints about you and other agents and then came my personal experience of you &c. &c. – which aided in his having a different opinion of you. You will therefore see it would do more harm than good my writing him. (SL 04/83: 1890, Sell's Box, HATa)

It is clear from this that Maddocks is acting informally to try and secure the clients' good opinion of Sell and that this involves a delicate balance. If Maddocks overplays his recommendation of Sell this would render an 'economic' basis to the transaction apparent and devalue the 'cultural' calculation of its worth.

These intricate entanglements between the 'cultural' and the 'economic' in the management of client relations also emerge in a memo from Jim Nance of General Motors to Howard Henderson of JWT regarding an unsuccessful presentation.

> [Y]our fellows just didn't have anyone that could make a speech. Do you know what I mean? In other words, you didn't have anyone who dished it out with any conviction ... there's something to the human emotions too – dishing it out to them (executives) is no different to dishing it out to salesmen ... I wouldn't want them [JWT management] to feel that the General Motors Corporation decided on an advertising agency too much on the way they presented their story but that's part of the agency business. (Howard Henderson file, 1935, Bernstein Company History Files, JWTa)

The memo provides a remarkable insight into some of the technical arrangements of presentations and into how decisions about the allocation of accounts were made. Although Nance is keen to avoid giving the impression that the decision was made on the strength of the style of the presentation, it is clear that JWT's presentation did not meet General Motor's expectations. Nance's memo goes on to explain that General Motors felt that JWT's market analysis was weak, that the JWT team 'didn't come in with any charts, their material was poorly gotten up'. This was a significant failing, Nance explains, because 'our organisation are just accustomed to talking that way'.

The salient point here is the extent to which this 'economic' judgement was a function of the tools JWT deployed to represent their analysis. Marketing charts are tools that shape or 'perform' the economic; they do not simply measure an economic 'reality' (Cochoy 1998; Law 2002). Marketing tools, as part of the discipline of marketing, define the practices and objects that constitute markets. This does not reduce to an argument that the market is socially constructed, but instead marks the ways in which specific marketing practices incorporate both economic 'science' and more cultural forms of managerial knowledge (Cochoy 1998). JWT's failure to win the account is thus neither a cultural nor an economic failure, but the result of differences between it and General Motors in both these dimensions of practice.

These illustrations of the constitutive interconnections between the economic and the cultural in the technical and organizational infrastructure of advertising are also evident in the development of media planning. This is a function that was carried out even in the earliest agencies. Agents like Barkers and Newton's in the early nineteenth century accepted advertising for any newspaper and provided a vital link to the volatile and rapidly changing newspaper industry through publishing lists of provincial newspapers (Charles Barker Letters Book 1825–47, CBa). By 1833, Barker's were describing themselves as agents of advertisers like the London and Westminster Bank and offering to keeps books of advertisements placed with their prices and locations and to check on all insertions (26 December 1833 Letter to London Westminster Bank, Charles Barker Letters Book 1825–47, CBa).

Newspaper directories published by agencies throughout the nineteenth and early twentieth centuries offer a useful insight into the development of media planning. By the 1840s, press directories were published by agents like Lewis and Lowe, whose list dates from 1844, and Charles Mitchell, who published his first *Newspaper Press Directory* in 1846 (Linton 1979, p. 29). In the 1860s, the agency Street's began publishing the *Indian and Colonial Mercantile Directory* and in 1885 Sell's published the first edition of its *Dictionary of the World's Press*. These and similar publications were updated regularly, often annually, and were an integral technical device in the practice of media planning. An indication of the types of use to which they were put can be gleaned from the style of entries. *The Times*, for instance, is described in Mitchell's first edition as:

> Daily, Price 5d. Established January 1 1788. ADVOCACY. High Church – Mercantile – Anti-New Poor Law – Anti-Corn Law. This the leading journal of Europe, has for the field of its circulation, emphatically, the WORLD, and its influence is coextensive with civilisation … *twenty thousand* impressions … (Mitchell 1846 in Linton 1979)

This engagement with the politics, religion, class and geography of newspapers and their readerships was a common feature of directories. Directories were devices that aided in the performance of media planning through making a form of order out of the complex and chaotic range of publications that carried advertising. Particular sorts of information about the press were ordered in particular ways, creating some possibilities and excluding others. This helped constitute and reinforce the cultural meanings attached to newspapers like *The Times* and in doing so helped define the economic value and price of advertising space in an irregular and haphazard market. Space rates set by newspapers in the UK and the US were negotiable and subject to large, capricious discounts (Linton 1979; Nevett 1982; Street's n.d.). Often 'the agent's column would be located alongside local advertising paying five and even ten times as much' (Raymond 1923 p. 18, JWTa). This anomalous system persisted because the absence of reliable circulation data made it extremely difficult for a uniform method of assessing the value of the space to be developed.[4] These circumstances were ideal for the development of a media specialism based on knowledge enshrined in the various competing agency press directories and by the end of the century media expertise was widely regarded as the core of advertising business, as in the following 1890s definition:[5]

> The businessman has an article he believes the multitude want, the question is how shall we apprise them of it in the smallest possible time, and in the least expensive manner? ... He knows the newspaper is the efficient means but which and when and how and where and last but not least what will it cost? are correlative questions which require knowledge and experience, and are not easily or quickly answered. This is the legitimate province of the advertising agent, and can be acquired only by special training and years of patience, industry, experience and skill. (Dodds in Raymond 1923, pp. 10–11, JWTa)

Space buying is often characterized as a basic service provided in an era where advertising functioned primarily to inform rather than persuade.[6] Viewed in this light, however, space buying is clearly a material practice that requires the exercise of both cultural judgement and economic calculation. Culture is not the context in which economic reality is embedded, rather categories such as price are simultaneously economically and culturally constituted. This emerges in specific instances of media-buying practice. Early agencies placed advertising not simply according to the status of the publication but also according to beliefs about the nature and habits of their readership and the degree of fit between them and the advertised product. Browne describes how selection of media in this period was based entirely on the familiarity agency space buyers acquired through continual study of the editorial content and advertisements in different newspapers (Browne, *c.* 1975, HATa). In 1897, for example, the agency Samson Clark advised Ogden's Tobacco to advertise a promotional competition in the halfpenny papers 'because we believe they are read more by the class of people who would be likely to take advantage of the advertisement' (Letter 25 November 1897, Samson Clark Box, HATa).

Selection of media, moreover, was only one aspect of agency service; also important were decisions about how advertising should be placed within the media. In an estimate of advertising space costs sent out by Sell's in 1888, for instance, papers are selected on the basis of their willingness to accept 'large display types' or 'blocks' and to position advertisements next to or surrounded by 'reading matter' (SL40, Sell's Box, HATa). This reflects the judgements practitioners made about how to secure maximum impact. The preference for blocks and display reflects their eye-catching capacity, but the desire to secure particular positions indicates a more subtle system of judgements about the value readers attached to different positions. This is evident in the following complaint sent by Samson Clark to *Ladies Field* in 1898.

> We received copy of *Ladies Field* yesterday and were not a little disgusted to find that three of the orders which we placed with you have been placed contrary to instructions. Messrs Debenham and Freebody's quarter page was to face matter on

the right hand page but it is on the left hand page in no position at all. Messrs Hampton and Sons half page was ordered for a right hand position, and if possible to face the last page of matter, it is on the left hand page and is under a very heavy advertisement of Fry's. Messr's Langley small advertisement was ordered specifically to go over Court and Society News – you have put it with the other small advertisements in no position at all! What are we to say to our clients? (Letter 18 March 1898, Samson Clark Box, HATa)

Media planning involves intricate decisions about reading practices and patterns of mental association between the nature of 'matter', competing advertisements and the advertisement placed. These decisions involve judgements, which are neither cultural nor economic, but necessarily both, as the economic value of space simply cannot be calculated outside of its cultural value.

This inextricability of cultural and economic elements is repeated again in instances of research practice. Research is the newest of the functional specialisms. It is of particular interest as the immediate, historical predecessor of the function of account planning, a methodological variant formulated in the 1960s to improve the articulation of research information with campaign production. Through incorporating the consumer's voice into creative strategy, planning has been accorded a central role in informing the production of a new generation of emotionally articulate advertisements (Nixon 1996). For Lash and Urry, account planning is an exemplary hybrid practice 'emblematic of the implosion of the economic, advertising as a business service, into the cultural, advertising as a "communications" or a "culture" industry' (1994, p. 141). Yet it is a function that can be traced in different forms at much earlier moments in the history of advertising practice.

The aims and methods employed in the earliest traceable research efforts varied enormously, but it is clear that by the mid-nineteenth century at least some clients and agencies had begun to recognize the value of using research to inform advertising. NW Ayer, for instance, undertook a market survey for a threshing machine manufacturer in 1879 (Hower 1939) while in 1891 JWT surveyed the face cream market for Ponds and in 1894 produced a campaign for Pabst Brewing Company based around an historical study of brewing (Account Files, JWTa). In 1903, JWT began testing consumer reactions to various advertising layouts by comparing the coupon responses to different advertisements placed for the same product (Raymond 1923, JWTa). This method of tracking the responses to advertisements placed in different publications through coded coupons was a technique which was attempted as far back as the 1850s (Nevett 1982, p. 52). The extent to which it was employed in this period is difficult to gauge, but by the early twentieth century it had become a cornerstone of the technique of 'scientific advertising' advanced by practitioners like Claud Hopkins, in his work at the agency Lord

& Thomas (Hopkins, 1990/1923). Scientific advertising, according to Hopkins, was 'based on fixed principles and according to fundamental laws. I learned those laws through thirty-six years of traced advertising. Through conducting campaigns on some hundreds of different lines. Through comparing, on some lines through keyed returns, thousands of pieces of copy' (1990/1923, p. 179). The approach emphatically stresses the importance of measuring advertising effectiveness and quantifying results. Hopkins believed that advertisements should be simple, sincere and provident; 'brilliant writing', persuasiveness and humour should be avoided at all costs (1990/1923, pp. 181–3).

Hopkins's views were extremely influential but they were far from the only principles guiding advertising production in this period. Other far less 'scientific' approaches to mapping the consumer were also adopted. One such practice was the distribution of products to staff members. At TB Browne's, for example, whenever more information about the qualities and uses of a product was sought it was distributed amongst appropriate staff members to provide a 'not scientific but practical' sample (Browne, c. 1975, p. 4, HATa). This practice continued long after more extensive research methods became available. In 1923 JWT used this approach in one of the first stages of a two year programme to launch Teba, a new Ponds shampoo.

> Samples of the first three experimental formulas for Pond's Liquid Castile Shampoo were distributed amongst members of our office, along with questionnaires on which they were asked to give their reactions to their sample ... Criticisms in these questionnaires were studied carefully and new formulas were worked out and new experiments made. (Cheseborough-Ponds file, 1923–26, Account Files, Box 3, JWTa)

This type of information gathering might be supposed to have been superseded by the development of more formal, economistic research instruments. Ethnographic studies of contemporary practitioners, however, continue to stress the centrality of practitioners' own idiosyncratic consumption habits and cultural references to the production process (Mort 1996, pp. 99–102; Nixon 1996, 2003). Indeed the possession and use of specific forms of aesthetic knowledge or what might be termed 'cultural capital' appears to have played an important role in the historical production of advertising (McFall 2002). Contemporary accounts of advertisers as an occupational group emphasize their atypicality as a predominantly young, well-resourced, well-educated and fashionable, urban elite (Mort 1996; Nixon, 1997, 2003), but such characteristics might equally be applied to much earlier generations of advertising producers (McFall 2002). The consumption practices of early advertising practitioners were in this way closely bound up with their work as producers.

Using agency staff as 'sovereign' consumers was not the only method agencies used to gather qualitative information about products. By the First World War, agencies like JWT and Ayer also sent staff out to work in department stores, replacing regular sales staff when they went on leave. There are numerous references to feedback derived in this way in JWT's account files for clients like Cheseborough-Ponds and the Andrew Jergens Company. These researchers were most often women, 'our girls', who would work as demonstrators to gather research information on products. Women were selected for this work specifically because of their perceived familiarity with the intimate knowledge, habits and desires of other women. An insight into the form this research information could take can be gleaned from the following:

> Miss Ashland acted as a Jergen's demonstrator and had some very interesting experiences. For instance we asked what really sold Violet Soap, and she said, 'Well, the coloured people come in, just one whiff of it and they cannot resist. (Cheseborough–Ponds file, 1923–26, Account Files, Box 3, JWTa)

Despite their sometimes idiosyncratic nature, staff reactions to products and experiences of consumers were regarded, institutionally, as of some consequence, and they fed back into the production process in a variety of ways. At the start of the twentieth century, the likelihood was that any research activity was undertaken by 'advertising all-rounders' who would also be involved in copy and layout production. By the end of the First World War, larger agencies had begun to employ specialist researchers who would participate in 'account groups' with account executives and creative staff. Even after research as a functional specialism had become more established in the late 1920s, however, agencies still stressed the value of sending copywriters out to 'regain their touch' by selling the product or observing its use. It was such 'hands-on' consumer mapping which sent Ayer's copywriter Dorothy Dignam to Europe to study housekeeping and to work in department stores.

The significance of such informal research knowledge in advertising practice is a little hard to judge. Agencies, unsurprisingly, have tended to emphasize their use of more formal research surveys and therefore date the beginning of research activity to the 1920s, when the techniques used began to resemble more closely those which became standard practice in the industry after 1945. Certainly by this time JWT, one of the main proponents of research, was using surveys and market investigation on an extensive and systematic basis. Between November 1922 and September 1923, JWT conducted 11 separate dealer and consumer investigations in the New York area for Woodbury's soap alone (Andrew Jergens Company, JWTa) while in the UK the company reputedly conducted 79 000 interviews for Ponds between 1923 and 1930 (Treasure 1977). JWT's 1959 account history omits mention of staff trials and selling experience for Ponds and describes how:

> From 1912–38, Pond's research in human behaviour was largely one-time quantitative consumer surveys. The earliest of these now on record was June 1927. It represented for the time a very advanced study of consumer purchasing behaviour, and included these research techniques which in recent years have been more fully developed.
>
> 1. What people do: how they use cosmetics
> 2. Why people do what they do: reason for using or not using cosmetic brands
> 3. People's awareness of and reaction to advertising
>
> (Cheseborough–Ponds file, 1959, Account Files, Box 3, JWTa)

Even a cursory glance at these 'very advanced' studies reveals the extent to which they were immersed in the meanings and values of the economically and culturally homogeneous occupational group which produced them. Segmentation on the basis of race, for instance, was routinely used. Research for the Cheek-Neal Company, makers of Maxwell House, split areas up according to 'the total number of families, number of native white families, number of negroes and foreign born' (Account Files, Box 3, JWTa). This information enabled surveys for companies like Jergen's to focus only on white families (Account Files, Box 1, JWTa). Consumer profiling on the basis of class was equally skewed. Product research for Arbuckle Brothers' coffee lines in 1912–13 for example, remarked that 'it is impossible to make each one of a line of products called by the same name, as strong as you can make a product which has a name of its own ... Consumers of the lower class can not be made to remember more than one name' (Account Files, Box 2, JWTa). Similarly a media plan for Cutex manicure products in 1926 was informed by the view that lower class interest in hand care was 'wholly negligible', although this was not a matter that the research investigation had actually addressed (Account Files, Box 3, JWTa). The imprint of the mainly female research interviewers' values on their findings is also strongly suggested in the interview summaries:

> Interview no.22 Young Irish girl with black hair and blue eyes – slovenly and very friendly ... The place has a rather frousy look ... She tried Woodbury's and stopped ... From the tone of her replies it is easy to deduce that price is a factor.
> Interview no. 52 Sickly, slovenly young woman with whisps of hair flying around her face and most of her front teeth missing. Stupid, preoccupied and overwrought. The house so new it smells of fresh timber and paint but it is already dirty and uninhabitable. This woman uses Ivory and Palmolive ... (Andrew Jergen's Company JWTa)

These research instruments and findings fit well with Cochoy's argument that the discipline of marketing acts to discipline markets through 'inventing special human and conceptual frames for market knowledge and practice' (1998, p. 194). This again is an illustration of the inadequacy of the increasing culturalization thesis as a description of the historical development of advertising practice. It is not simply that this early advertising research could be construed as cultural in the sense invoked by Lash and Urry (1994), Mort (1996) and Nixon (1997) – that its specific aim was to bring the 'cultural' voice of consumers into the advertising process. This restricts culture to the representational domain. The more substantial difficulty is that research practice, as with media planning, account management and all other forms of material practice, is unthinkable outside of its cultural constitution.

In a range of different ways, the non-creative functional specialisms– account management, media planning and research – illustrate the irreducibility of working practices to the economic or the cultural. In each specialism, aspects of everyday work are contingent upon the exercise of judgements which are simultaneously economic and cultural. The contention is thus that the economic and the cultural should be understood as elements that together constitute practice. This questions the value of thinking in terms of the increasing 'culturalization' of work in the information/knowledge economy, as advertising's past simply does not, on close examination, stand up to its idealization as an era where culture was sealed off from the economics of daily business. Yet the work involved in the production of advertising not only spotlights the imbrication of culture and economy but also the articulation of production and consumption. The work of advertising producers necessarily calls upon their experiences as 'sovereign' consumers to reflect upon, describe and ultimately promote products. To this extent their identities as workers are simultaneous with and interdependent upon their identities as consumers.

CONCLUDING COMMENTS

This chapter set out, first, to review arguments that work and working identities have been subject to a series of profound transformations as part of the shift towards a new information- or knowledge-based society. Such arguments form part of a vast and diverse body of literature relating to the character or condition of the epoch which in no way presents a single, unified picture of the nature of contemporary change. Nevertheless an effort has been made to establish the persistence of certain themes in this literature in regard to transformations in economic organization, production and work and to corresponding changes in culture, consumption and leisure. At the most general level, substantive global economic restructuring occasioned by an increasing dependence on knowledge/information resources, is interpreted as evidence of the shift to what is variously described – among other terms – as 'post', 'second' or 'reflexive' modernity. One of the key processes defining this new modernity is individualization. While concern with processes of individualization stretches back to nineteenth century thinkers, a more recent generation of thinkers, including Castells, Beck and Lash and Urry, use the term to invoke a shift from the social and collective to the individual. A whole panoply of changes can be accommodated under this rubric, from individually negotiated work contracts, decentralized management structures, empowered and enterprising employees to small batch production and customized 'niche' markets. The process of individualization thus carries serious implications for the nature of work and work-based identity. Crucially it is individualization that seems to underpin the increasing redundance of work as the basis of identity and its perceived replacement by consumption. It is the broad process of individualization, for Lash and Urry (1994), that frees consumption from the structuring influence of social, family and corporate groups, allowing (or forcing) individuals to use their lifestyles and consumer choices to construct their identities.

It should by now be clear that such accounts tend to approach their analyses of contemporary change in fairly dualistic terms. Oppositions are set up between past and present; between economy, production and work, and culture; between consumption and leisure. Thus, in some accounts, society in general and work in particular are understood to be subject to a process of 'culturalization' as the very principle of more information intensive industrial production. In another variant of epochal theory, 'autonomous' culture appears as a casualty, forever at the devaluative service of economic imperatives in an increasingly branded and commercialized world. Whichever version is preferred, it is clear that culture and economy are supposed, normatively, to be separate domains – their de-differentiation is a contemporary aberration. Yet a general analytic distinction between culture and economy, it was proposed, is surprisingly difficult to apply in instances of material practice. Some theorists have posited an alternative model of culture as a situated and contingent category whose limited and technical forms are best considered as existing only through specific historical arrangements, institutions and practices. Thus the economic and the cultural can be understood as *performed* in material practice under particular arrangements and utilizing particular socio-technical devices. This informed the approach taken to the study of advertising as a constituent material practice – a term intended to signal the impossibility of a purely economic form of business practice.

Advertising was taken as a useful empirical starting point because its apparently mediative place between production and consumption/culture and economy has accorded it a consequential role in general, critical accounts of the post-industrial or information/knowledge age. Considered as a constituent material practice, historical advertising offers an alternative to the invocation of an idealized past in which economy and culture existed in a more bounded sealed-off state. By offering a different perspective on the intercalibration of culture and economy in the everyday working practices of a range of historical practitioners, the example of advertising casts doubt on generalized arguments about the culturalization of work. It also serves to illustrate some of the interconnections between production and consumption. Practitioners in the past, just like their contemporary counterparts, relied heavily on their consumption and lifestyle experiences in the conduct of their work. This entanglement of consumption and production hints at one of the problems of forecasting a wholesale shift to consumption rather than work as the primary means through which to negotiate identity. It is, however, far from the only problem. A much more intransigent difficulty lies with the protean character of identity itself. The corollary of the widespread, if not quite universal, rejection in social theory of the notion of a fixed and transhistorical essence to identity is acceptance that identity is a multi-faceted, shifting and contingent phenomenon. Indeed, as Rose (1998, p. 4) has suggested, the ideal of the 'unified, coherent, self-centred subject' not only conceals a more diverse empirical reality but has perhaps its greatest purchase in projects that lament the loss of the true self in modern life. It is not too great a leap of faith to place pronouncements of the demise of work-based identity in this category. Identity is best understood as expressed through historical, technical means which include work and consumption among a host of other variables. Identity is thus always, necessarily contingent upon the vast assemblage of techniques, practices and strategies through which subjects are enjoined to relate to and make sense of themselves (Rose 1998; du Gay *et al.* 2000). From this vantage point it makes little sense to read shifts in the foundations of identity from work to consumption from the character of the epoch. In instances of material, historical practice things are seldom as neatly demarcated as they appear when marshalled as the objects of generalizing, critical theory.

NOTES

1. These themes can be found in various forms in the work of Beck (2000), Castells (2000), Gorz (1999), Rifkin (1995), Ritzer (1998), Sennett (1998) and Smart (2003).
2. See Miller and Rose (1990), Allen and du Gay (1994) and du Gay (1996).
3. The claim to provide an essential 'professional' service is a familiar theme in the trade literature of this period. J.Walter Thompson's 1899: *Red Book*; Sell's 1908: *The Propelling Power*; Spottiswoode's 1909: *The Triangle*, are amongst numerous examples.
4. In the US the Audit Bureau of Circulations was established in 1914 whilst the British Audit Bureau of Circulations was not set up until 1933. Prior to this, newspapers published their

own data but its reliability was extremely variable.
5. Curiously, a similar logic of market pluralization has been used to explain the phenomena of specialist 'media-buying' agencies which occurred in the late 1980s (compare Lash and Urry, 1994, p. 141; Nixon, 1996, p. 110–14).
6. See for instance Leiss *et al.* (1990).

REFERENCES

Allen, J. and P. du Gay (1994), 'Industry and the Rest: The Economic Identity of Service Services', *Work, Employment and Society*, **8** (2), 255–71.
Baudrillard, J. (1988), 'Consumer Society', in M. Poster (ed.), *Selected Writings*, Cambridge: Polity Press.
Bauman, Z. (1998), *Work, Consumerism and the New Poor*, Buckingham: Open University Press.
Bauman, Z. (2001), 'Consuming Life', *Journal of Consumer Culture*, **1** (1), 9–29.
Beck, U. (2000), *The Brave New World of Work*, Cambridge: Polity Press.
Beck, U., A. Giddens and S. Lash (1994), *Reflexive Modernization, Politics, Tradition and Aesthetics in Modern Social Theory*, Cambridge: Polity Press.
Bell, D. (1973), *The Coming of Post-Industrial Society*, London: Heinemann.
Buck-Morss, S. (1995), 'Envisioning Capital: Political Economy on Display', *Critical Inquiry*, Winter, 434–67.
Callon, M. (ed.) (1998), *The Laws of the Market*, Oxford: Blackwell.
Callon, M., C. Meadel and V. Rabeharisoa (2002), 'The Economy of Qualities', *Economy and Society*, **31** (2), 194–217.
Castells, M. (1997), *The Power of Identity*, vol. 2 of *The Information Age: Economy, Society and Culture*, Oxford: Blackwell.
Castells, M. (1998), *The End of Millennium*, vol. 3 of *The Information Age: Economy, Society and Culture*, Oxford: Blackwell.
Castells, M. (2000), *The Rise of the Network Society*, vol. 1 of *The Information Age: Economy, Society and Culture*, 2nd edn, Oxford: Blackwell.
Cochoy, F. (1998), 'Another Discipline for the Market Economy: Marketing as a Performative Knowledge and Know-how for Capitalism', in M. Callon (ed.), *The Laws of the Market*, Oxford: Blackwell.
Davis, H. and R. Scase, (2000), *Managing Creativity: The Dynamics of Work and Organisation*, Buckingham: Open University Press.
du Gay, P. (1996), *Consumption and Identity at Work*, London: Sage.
du Gay, P. and M. Pryke (eds) (2002), *Cultural Economy*, London: Sage.
du Gay, P., J. Evans and P. Redman (eds) (2000), *Identity in Question*, London: Sage.
Featherstone, M. (1991), *Consumer Culture and Postmodernism*, London: Sage.
Gorz, A. (1999) *Reclaiming Work: Beyond the Wage Based Society*, Cambridge: Polity Press.
Hall, S. (ed.) (1997), *Representation*, London: Sage.
Hopkins, C. (1990) [1929 and 1923], *My Life in Advertising and Scientific Advertising: Two Works by Claud Hopkins*, Chicago: NTC Business Books.
Hower, R. (1939) *The History of an Advertising Agency*, New York: Arno.
Lash, S. and J. Urry (1987), *The End of Organised Capitalism*, Cambridge: Polity Press.
Lash, S. and J. Urry (1994), *Economies of Signs and Space*, London: Sage.
Law, J. (2002), 'Economics as Interference', in P. du Gay and M. Pryke (eds), *Cultural*

Economy, London: Sage.
Leiss, W., S. Kline and S. Jhally (1990), *Social Communication in Advertising*, 2nd edn, London: Routledge.
Linton, D. (1979), 'Mr Mitchell's National Work', *Journal of Advertising History*, **2**, January, 29–31.
McFall, L. (2002), 'What About the Old Cultural Intermediaries? An Historical Review of Advertising Producers', *Cultural Studies*, **16** (4), 532–53.
Mattelart, A. (1991), *Advertising International: The Privatisation of Public Space*, London: Routledge.
Miller, P. (2001), 'Governing by Numbers: Why Calculative Practices Matter', *Social Research*, **68** (2), 379–96.
Miller, P. and N. Rose (1990), 'Governing Economic Life', *Economy and Society*, **19** (1), 1–31.
Moeran, B. (1996), *A Japanese Advertising Agency*, Surrey: Curzon.
Mort, F. (1996), *Cultures of Consumption*, London: Routledge.
Nevett, T. (1982), *Advertising in Britain*, London: Heinemann.
Nixon, S. (1996), *Hard Looks: Masculinities, Spectatorship and Contemporary Consumption*, London: UCL Press Ltd.
Nixon, S. (1997), 'Circulating Culture', in P. du Gay (ed.), *Production of Culture/ Cultures of Production*, London: Sage.
Nixon, S. (2003) *Advertising Cultures: Gender, Commerce, Creativity*, London: Sage.
Ray, L. and A. Sayer (1999), *Culture and Economy after the Cultural Turn*, London: Sage.
Rifkin, J. (1995), *The End of Work*, London: Penguin.
Ritzer, G. (1998), *The McDonaldization Thesis*, London: Sage.
Rose, N. (1998), *Inventing Ourselves: Psychology, Power and Personhood*, Cambridge: Cambridge University Press.
Sennett, R. (1998), *The Corrosion of Character: The Personal Consequences of Work in the New Capitalism*, New York, London: W.W. Norton.
Sennett, R. (2001), 'Street and Office: Two Sources of Identity', in W. Hutton and A. Giddens (eds), *On the Edge: Living With Global Capitalism*, London: Vintage.
Smart, B. (2003), *Economy, Culture and Society*, Buckingham: Open University Press.
Toffler, A. (1970), *Future Shock*, New York: Random House.
Touraine, A. (1974), *The Post-Industrial Society*, New York: Wildwood Press.
Turner, C. (1992), *Modernity and Politics in the Work of Max Weber*, London: Routledge.
Wernick, A. (1991), *Promotional Culture: Advertising, Ideology and Symbolic Expression*, London: Sage.

PRIMARY SOURCES

Abbreviations

HATa – History of Advertising Trust Archives, Norwich.
JWTa – J. Walter Thompson Archive, Hartman Center, Duke University, North Carolina.
CBa – Charles Barker Archive, Guildhall Library, London.

Account files, Boxes 1, 2, 3, 6 and 13, JWTa.
Andrew Jergen's Company, Roll 45, Market Research microfilms, JWTa.
Charles Barker Letters Book 1825–47 MS 20011, CBa.
Bernstein Company History Files, Biographical File Series, Box 4, JWTa.
Browne, Reginald Bousquet (*c.* 1975). *T.B. Browne Limited: The First 100 Years*, Unpublished memoir, Agencies Box, HATa.
Dawkins Papers: Officers and Staff series, Box 1, 3, JWTa.
Kohl, Howard (1956), Kohl celebrates 50 years with JWT in *Round the Square*, Dawkins Papers, Officers and Staff series, Box 2 JWTa.
Norris, Ernest (1967), *From Memories*, Internal memoir, Sell's Box, HATa.
Raymond, Charles E. (1923), *Memoirs and Reminiscences*, Unpublished manuscript, Officers and Staff series Box 1, JWTa.
Samson Clark Box, HATa.
Sell's Guardbook, 1891, Sell's Box, HATa.
Sell's Services Presentation document c.1910 SL53, Sells Box, HATa.
Sell's List of Suburban Newspapers (1888) Sells Box, HATa.
SL/04/83, Sell's Box, HATa.
SL40, Sell's Box, HATa.
Spottiswoode's *The Triangle* (1909), Spottiswoode's Box, HATa.
Streets (n.d.). *The Story of Streets*, Unpublished Manuscript.
Treasure, J.A.P. (1977), *A History of British Advertising Agencies*, Edinburgh University Jubilee Lecture, HATa.

2. Changing times, changing identities: a case study of British journalists
Gill Ursell

> (We) are concerned less with advancing a simple historical narrative of changing ideas about the 'person' than with focusing upon the social relations, techniques, and forms of training and practice through which individuals have acquired definite capacities and attributes for social existence as particular 'sorts' of people. This ... involves an historical understanding of the limited and specific forms of 'personhood' that individuals acquire in their passage through social institutions.
> (du Gay *et al.* 2000, p. 279)

The analytical position indicated above encapsulates the approach to identity taken in this chapter, that is, social relational and empirically grounded. This distinguishes it from the essentially theoretical analyses of writers such as Rose (1998, 1999), Giddens (1990, 1991) and Beck (1992), who make assertions about individual identity formation in the context of their broader theorizations of a significantly changed social world, namely, the 'post' or 'late' or 'second' modern. These analyses are stimulating and valuable in their own right, but to test empirically the strength of their propositions about individuals *qua* individuals is to run the risk of an ethnographic methodology which renders social generalizations problematic. A further reason to prefer a social relational and grounded approach is the suspicion that the focus of much contemporary social theory on individualization is itself an element of the self-actualization discourse which it purports to be analysing. This suspicion seems also to inform Castells's preference (1997) for a socially contextualized approach to identity.

Castells defines identity as 'people's source of meaning and experience' (1997, p. 6), and sees it as being formulated socially in relation to collectives of others whose features are of particular salience. He proposes a three-fold categorization of identity, namely: 'legitimizing identity', to do with membership of a polity such as the nation-state; 'resistant identity', to do with membership of a community distinct from other collectives; and 'project identity', to do with the individual's techniques of adaptation and self-government. It is in the latter conception that Castells comes closest to the perspectives on identity of writers such as Giddens, Rose and Beck. But

Castells is distinct from these authors in his hypothesis that, where under contemporary conditions there is any collapse of a sense of citizenship and membership of a viable polity, individuals will resort less to their own inner selves and more to communities of perceived similar others. Thus, against assertions of the 'individualizing' structures of the new world, Castells is positing a much stronger place for communally-based forms of identity and resistance. This bears a happy coincidence with Johnson's (1972) argument that the claim to a certain identity (in his illustration, being a 'professional') should be recognized as a technique for negotiating status and place in society, the success of which is contingent upon the strengths and preferences of those with whom the negotiations are conducted.

The empirical focus of this chapter, on British journalists and their occupational identity, is an attempt to demonstrate the strength of Castells's and Johnson's analyses in the narrow context of this one type of occupation. This is because many of the theorizations of the new world lay claim to the emergence of a new breed of worker, one who specializes in information and in networking. This new breed is seen to be created in the transformative influences of electronic technologies on the recrafting of capitalist enterprise as genuinely global corporations, in the accelerated process of capitalist intrusion into all parts of the globe, and in the production of information as a vendible commodity. The argument advanced below is that journalists have been information networkers since their emergence with the Gutenberg printing press in the 15th century. They cannot therefore readily be construed as a new breed. Nonetheless, the 'old' breed of journalists has experienced considerable occupational change over the centuries. It is the aim of this chapter to reveal the changing roles, norms and practices of journalism as applied within and by the power structures which are the social context for journalist identity formation. It is proposed below that, by early 19th century in Britain, the occupational identity of journalists was initially constructed as 'legitimizing' but that the specificities of this legitimizing identity subsequently became an identity of 'resistance'. Following from this, in section three, the contemporary conditions under which journalists now operate will be described. These conditions will be weighed against certain themes arising from theorizations of a new breed of workers, and they will be proposed to represent structural changes which are 'individualizing' only for the few. That is, individualizing 'project' identity formation is seen to be the condition for only a minority of journalists.

To address the issues, primary data was drawn from in-depth interviews conducted in the first half of 2002 with press, broadcast and online journalists in Britain and Canada. To reduce the weight of detail, however, attention is given primarily to the British experience. However, the Canadian data suggest strong parallels with the British experience. The total number of interviewees was small (19 in Britain, 12 in Canada) but sufficient in the context of a broad range of secondary research data, and an extensive literature search. The author also works alongside trainee journalists in her full-time professional capacity; these newcomer journalists (around 30 per annum) have allowed observation of identity formation under contemporary conditions.

THE INSTITUTIONALIZATION OF JOURNALISTS AS THE FOURTH ESTATE: A 'LEGITIMIZING IDENTITY'

Journalists played a significant role in the forging of the modern state and the discursive norms, practices and organizational mechanisms enfolding successive sections of the population into democratic society. As such, journalism can be identified closely with the political and cultural ambitions of the modernist project, understood as a set of goals which combines the political enfranchisement of the masses with their intellectual, cultural and welfare enrichment. The modernist project advanced in Western Europe in the context of the Enlightenment's optimism about scientific method and reasoning. Given that context, it is hardly surprising that the originating practices and values of journalism reveal modernist principles prescribing a dispassionate approach to the systematic and rigorous establishment of facts, and a public approach to their evaluation. Moreover, the definition of news in the foundational days reflected very strongly a concern for political events and powerful élites. The nascent press, established in Britain from the 16th century, was substantially political in its contents: indeed it attracted state suppression (firstly from Henry VIII, subsequently from Oliver Cromwell). But by 1702, Samuel Buckley, as editor of the very first daily national newspaper (*Daily Courant*) was clear that the task of his paper was to 'give news, not views'. 'Views' became the speciality of his second publication in 1712. His title, *The Spectator*, was to be 'an elegant coffee-house periodical for gentlefolk ... to bring philosophy out of the closets and libraries, schools and colleges, to dwell in clubs and assemblies, at tea-tables and in all coffee houses' (Newspaper Society 1997). Politics and philosophy were the idealized news agenda of early 18th century Britain.

Subsequently Habermas (1974, 1979, 1984) described these developments in Britain and Western Europe as the emergence of a 'public sphere', enabling informed and rationally reflected public debate about the issues of the day. This concept of a public sphere and its modes of address involves an identification of journalists as individuals moving freely in society, enabled to report the facts fully and accurately, conscientiously discriminating between representations of fact and representations of opinion, and working to news agenda defined by the public interest. This identification did not wait upon

Habermas but was captured in Carlyle's famous invocation (1840, p. 194) of journalists as the Fourth Estate of the Realm.

It can be suggested that Carlyle's portrayal constitutes a general social acceptance of journalists as having privileged institutional status in the mechanisms of developing democracy. They had achieved, that is, a legitimating identity in Castells's sense. Further evidence of that acceptability and status can be drawn from Queen Victoria's award of a Royal Charter to the Institute of Journalists in 1890. The political importance of journalism in the establishment of the modern state is further demonstrated in the part played by English journalist and author of *The Rights of Man* (1791), Tom Paine, in the writing of the Bill of Rights defining the constitution of a newly independent America. Indeed, in Canada the establishment of a free press is said to have preceded that of the nation (Desbarats 1996).

THE PROFESSIONALIZATION OF JOURNALISM: A 'RESISTANT IDENTITY'

The existence of a press independent of the state has come to be a major signifier of democracy, and any moves on the part of politicians towards state intervention have typically been deflected by reference to this signification. But in these same 18th and 19th centuries, the state-free press was also constructed as an economic enterprise in five major aspects: a) as a site of employment for journalists; b) as a source of tax revenue for governments; c) as a vehicle and interpreter of market information; d) as an economic base for political power; and e) as a commodity, the sales of which could be enhanced by journalism practices antithetical to Fourth Estate norms. That is, from the 18th century, the heroic and 'legitimizing' identity of journalists as the Fourth Estate was being challenged on the evidence that some journalists were being employed to produce stories and to conduct themselves in ways antithetical to that identity. Indeed, the creation of the Institute of Journalists (IOJ) can be regarded as evidence of journalists' efforts to counter, as an occupational community, the pressures towards what were, in their understanding of their social and political significance, lower standards. The Institute described and describes itself as working to encourage the highest possible standards, and to represent individuals 'at the top of their profession' (http://www.ioj.co.uk).

The Institute's view of journalism as a profession, in the sense of a dispassionate and conscientious servant of the public, accompanied a commitment to negotiate with employers rather than confront them. As such, the Institute differs from the National Union of Journalists (NUJ), founded in 1907, which describes itself explicitly as a 'wage earners' union'. The NUJ is as much concerned with standards as is the IOJ, and the IOJ is as much concerned with wages and conditions of employment as is the NUJ. The difference between the two organizations is essentially one of perceived identity and affiliation. For the IOJ, the journalist is a professional, different from the labouring classes, who should not be linked by union membership to the broader labour movement or Labour Party. For the NUJ, the journalist is an employee who, notwithstanding professional responsibilities, can expect to be overridden by editors and exploited by proprietors, and whose best interests therefore lie in collective action via the labour movement and the Labour Party. It must be said that the NUJ is the larger and better known of the two organizations. Its membership presently comprises 58 per cent of all journalists working in the United Kingdom, and it is the world's largest journalist union.

The 20th century in Britain is distinguished by conflicts between proprietorial use of journalists, on the one hand, and journalists' occupational perceptions on the other, with the collective organizations of the NUJ and IOJ acting as their representatives in national and local fora of debate and negotiation. The NUJ's official historian, F. J. Mansfield (1943), comments on the union's concerns from its inception about the compromise of journalism standards by commercial pressures for sensationalist and scurrilous story telling and by requirements to intrude into grief and privacy, leading in 1936 to the introduction of the NUJ's Code of Professional Conduct (Frost 2000, p. 224). As Harcup (2001, p. 4) describes, in 1917 the NUJ was being asked by its Central London branch to act 'as the guardian of the profession's honour', and in 1931 a union member who suffered for refusing to carry out instructions 'repugnant to his sense of dignity' was promised the union's moral and financial support. The Code adopted in 1936 at the Annual Delegate Meeting pledged union backing for journalists who refused to do work 'incompatible with the honour and interests of the profession'. NUJ members were instructed not to falsify information or misrepresent facts, and were warned by the Code, 'Whether for publication or suppression, the acceptance of a bribe by a journalist is one of the gravest professional offences' (O'Mally and Soley 2000, p. 43). Fifty years later, in 1986, reflecting the lack of real change from proprietors, the NUJ established its own Ethics Council (Frost 2000, p. 224; Harcup 2002), to educate members and help promote better standards, and to hear complaints against members alleged to have breached the Code.

The NUJ and the IOJ were not alone in preferring the view of journalists as professionals. The NUJ's membership of the Trades Union Congress gave it a significant voice in the labour movement, on which the power of the Labour Party was structured. At the initiative of two journalists who had become Labour MPs (Frost 2000, p. 176), the concern for standards was taken up by the Labour government returned to office at the close of the Second World War. This government set up the first Royal Commission on the Press, the remit of which was 'how journalistic conduct [could] be restrained and reformed, how newspaper culture [could] be improved and how the range of publications [could] be protected or widened' (Tulloch 1998, p. 71). As Tulloch comments, all discussion and decision making was stymied by the equation of the free press with the free market, Conservative opposition and press proprietors arguing fiercely for the latter while Labour politicians were afraid to be seen to compromise the former. Nonetheless, the NUJ's proposal for the establishment of a Press Council was adopted as a recommendation of the Commission and, in 1953, the proprietors eventually conceded to political pressure and established it. Described as a 'toothless watchdog' by many (Robertson 1983; O'Malley and Soley 2000, p. 79), by the late 1970s, after two further Royal Commissions into the Press, the Press Council was nonetheless publishing criticism of practices such as 'cheque book journalism' and 'trial by newspaper'.

Nevertheless, throughout the 1980s, the national tabloid newspapers were involved in numerous instance of poor quality journalism, leading to the parliamentary establishment of the Calcutt Committee in 1989 to investigate invasions of privacy by journalists. The Committee called for more stringent self-regulation by proprietors and editors, with a two-year probationary period to prove they could do it. The second Calcutt Committee reviewing matters in 1991, concluded that not enough had been done, and recommended statutory interventions. None were made; however, the Press Council was reconstituted in that year, with government acceptance, as a Press Complaints Commission (PCC). This, observes Tulloch (1998, p. 79), was set up as a customer complaints mechanism and as such, it deflected attention from the employment of journalists and the economic forces they faced.

Thus for British newspaper journalists, the 20th century was one in which they came together as an occupational community to create central organizations which defined high professional standards, which attempted to oversee and uphold them, and which negotiated on their behalf with employers and with governments. We can regard this as the effort of journalists to create a singular professional identity, one which in its honouring might ensure job satisfaction, one which might inculcate norms and good practices among members, and one which could stand as a defensive mechanism against unhelpful pressures from employers. But, as Johnson points out (1972), the status of 'professional' is a measure of the success of the claim to that status, not a measure of attributes of the occupation. In this particular instance, the journalists' effort to claim and to realize a professional identity was treated by many employers as irrelevant. Moreover, the degree of institutionalization of journalism as a Fourth Estate was unpicked sufficiently to allow free market arguments to dominate. The 1986 adoption of a consumer complaint model for the PCC can be taken as the turning point away from political commitments to journalism 'in the public interest' and towards journalism 'of interest to the public'. The historical legacy of the Fourth Estate model of journalism remains only, but importantly, as a 'resistant identity' in the terms defined by Castells.

A shorter but essentially parallel development has taken place in British broadcasting. From broadcasting's inception as a public service, its journalists have operated within precise guidelines under the direction of managerial hierarchies accountable to Parliament. But government concern for the economic efficiency of the British Broadcasting Corporation led to interventions of management consultants in the mid-1970s. Faced with the prospect of non-broadcasting people influencing work practices and outcomes, different sections of the BBC resorted to claims of their professional superiority. As Burns reports (1977), the claim to professionalism became a 'semantic credit card'. With regard to BBC journalists, the credit card carried Fourth Estate details as interpreted by the first Director-General, Lord John Reith, that is, news as a public service, politically neutral, dispassionately delivered and factually comprehensive.

Interestingly, Burns found a different credit card being utilized by BBC employees working in light entertainment programming. This group defined their professionalism in terms of abilities to attract and hold audience attention. This is significant because, in the 1980s, British governments moved towards a less state-regulated, more market-regulated model for British broadcasting; one in which the BBC remains the cornerstone of public service but in which there is increasingly intense competition for audiences and revenues. A journalistic ability to 'tickle the punter' has accordingly risen in value for the broadcasting employers, leading to alternative definitions of professional identity among journalists and, from some quarters, protestations of 'dumbing down' (for example Franklin 1997; Bromley 2001). The accusation is that standards of journalism have fallen in two senses: one, in the trivializing of the news agenda and two, in the development of personality-led news presentation. A third form of complaint, of explicit bias in Fox TV news coverage of the Iraqi invasion, was recently dismissed by the Independent Television Commission as not relevant in the context of consumer choice.

The various aspects of change affecting both press and broadcast journalists, posing questions for their professionalism and how to define it, inform substantially the many higher education courses through which journalists nowadays enter the industry. Research by the Journalism Training Forum (2002) found 96 per cent of British journalists to be graduates or postgraduates, a fact which further reinforces the representation of journalists as professionals, but which does not automatically indicate how this professional identity is to be defined. What we can see, however, in the statements of the National Union of Journalists, the Institute of Journalists, the Press Complaints Commission and recurrent parliamentary debates about standards of news reporting, is the frequent articulation of concerns that the professionalism of journalists as the Fourth Estate is under increasing threat from commercial and political factors. The inherited 'legitimating identity' of the Fourth Estate is thus now constructed as the 'resistant identity' of journalists as professionals.

JOURNALISTS IN THE 21ST CENTURY

Journalists of both press and broadcasting may not be a new breed of information worker, but over the years they have experienced substantial change in the nature of their work. Changes have taken place in the agendas to which they work, in the styles of presentation, in the media of presentation, in the technologies of production, in the organization and division of labour, in the manufacturing processes of news production, and in the institutional status of the ethics and standards of journalism practice. Thus it may be that it is the emergent role and status of journalists, rather than the breed, which is new. To explore this possibility, it is helpful to take from the literature the various conceptualizations of the new breed of worker.

For Nixon (1997), Negus (1997) and Bourdieu (1986, 1998), the new world is one in which 'cultural intermediaries' make a significant contribution. This concept of 'cultural intermediary' denotes a worker whose job tasks insert him/her into the social and organizational processes by which much of contemporary western culture is produced. Nixon's use of the concept is particular to his analysis of the work of advertisers, marketeers and public relations personnel, but Negus does also identify journalists (1997, p. 98). In their analysis, the promotional or commercial character of much of western culture is linked to the job specifications and performances of these 'cultural intermediary' workers. This is an occupational category which is essential to the production and reproduction of consumerist culture.

A different approach is that of the French sociologist, Pierre Bourdieu. Bourdieu (1986) identifies the growth of a class of cultural intermediaries and regards them as a new petite bourgeoisie, a new lower middle class. These people are, he says, free-thinking, not necessarily employed or formally qualified, not necessarily wealthy, but certainly knowledgeable and opinionated on cultural matters and, being skilled in the use of the media, publicly so. Their class may include journalists, but is not limited to them. In Bourdieu's account, cultural intermediary workers can demonstrate a significant degree of autonomy from the structures and values of contemporary capitalism. But journalists working for media corporations are unlikely to; they are, in Bourdieu's terms, 'the day labourers of everyday life' (1998, p. 7).

An alternative conception is that of Robert Reich (1991), who proposes the new élite occupational category of 'symbolic analysts'. These are the jet-setting, globe-trotting, nouveau riche who not only use the electronic infrastructure on a 24/7 basis, but who are in command of the meanings, information and business transactions which flow globally through it and which constitute the very stuff of late capitalist enterprise and culture. Below this new élite are two other strata, those who undertake routine production services, and those who provide in-person services. Relevant here is the global mobility of the symbolic analysts relative to the localized relative immobility of the others.

There are similarities between Reich's proposals and those of Castells (1996) who talks of 'networkers' as the cultural and entrepreneurial decision makers of the 'network society'. They are joined in 'network society' by a middle layer of support workers who implement but do not make significant decisions, and a bottom layer who are acted upon and who, if they have jobs, will be in receipt of employment instructions from above.

Lyotard's (1984) focus similarly discriminates between new élite workers and the rest. He talks of the impact of science and technology on communications, granting a simultaneous capacity for symbolic manipulation and a capacity to displace human labour. This leads, he proposes, to the emergence of a professional intelligentsia (doctors, lawyers, and so on) who will govern, and a technical intelligentsia (scientists, engineers, and so on) who will ensure continued and substantial change in the material conditions of existence. These people are relatively few and for them there will be the best forms of liberal (that is, full range) education. For everyone else, there will be vocational education (much of it centring on computer-based information gathering and processing) intent on imparting employment skills and, in particular, the values and practice of 'performativity'. Individual workers at this level are to be employed and rewarded only to the extent that it can be demonstrated that they add value to production outcomes. The broad swathe of computer-literate, mental workers of the 21st century displace the manual workers of earlier times as the base line of the workforce – 'the day labourers of everyday life', as Bourdieu puts it (1998).

Have journalists become 'the day labourers of everyday life'? Are they 'cultural intermediaries' helping to reproduce consumerist culture? Are they among the new information elites? Are the conceptualizations adequate? To address these questions, British journalists' experiences are weighed below against certain thematic concerns recurrent in the conceptualizations: namely, the social and cultural role of the occupation; its autonomy and status; and job-related mobility.

THE SOCIAL AND CULTURAL ROLE OF JOURNALISTS

The number of journalists in Britain has risen sharply over recent years, from around 40000 in the late 1980s (IMS 1989) to 60000, with the anticipation of continued increase such that by 2010 there could be 80000 to 90000 (Journalism Training Forum 2002). The rise is accounted for by two main factors. One is that there is now a much broader range of occupations where journalism skills are sought. The promotional and commercial activities of contemporary capitalism are realized in the rise of public communication practices and jobs in central and local government, in corporations, public services, charitable bodies, sports and media organizations themselves. The first beginnings of this rise can be traced back to the 1940s but it has accelerated substantially in more recent decades.

The second factor is the advent of new media and growth in number and output of traditional media. By any measure, Britain is a media-rich country. The annually updated *Willings Press Guide* lists for 2002 a total UK media count of 17 963 publications (all media). On any one day in Britain, *Willings* shows the average daily national papers sold to total 13 389 711. To these must be added the audited websites of the major newspapers and broadcasters (Stokes and Reading 1999, p.120). For example, hit rates (that is number of page impressions visited) for BBC Online have been in excess of 12 million per month since early 1998, and are in excess of 5 million per month for each of ITN Online, *The Times* and the *Sunday Times*.

There is, however, substantial argument as to the qualities and purposes of this profusion. The catch phrase 'dumbing down' captures the accusations. For some observers, journalism output is seen to reveal a fresh or accelerated deterioration of standards. The arguments are less to do with bad conduct by journalists and more to do with growth in coverage of that which is trivial, superficial and/or salacious relative to shrinking proportions of coverage of the serious, the worthy, the challenging. It is seen to be the adoption of presentation styles that stress dynamic action, star personalities and informality over more sober, dispassionate and analytical treatments. It is identified with the growing weight of media attention to sports, show business, consumption and the aspirational fancies of its audiences as individuals (for example, Franklin 1997; Barnett and Seymour 1999; Bromley 2001). Journalism is seen now to be engaged in prioritizing and extolling self-indulgence and self-concern to the neglect of attention to issues of the social good and public well-being (for example Dahlgren and Sparks 1991; Stephenson and Bromley 1998). It is viewed as a threat to the workings of the public sphere (for example Morley 2000).

Such evidence and reflection on changes in journalism performance inevitably raise questions over its contemporary social and cultural role. Is it any longer to facilitate the public sphere? Or is there here evidence supportive of the thesis of Lash and Urry (1994) that changes in media performance reveal the emergence of 'economies of signs and space' appropriate to the needs of late consumer capitalism? If we believe there is, then we can represent journalists as 'cultural intermediaries' in the sense defined by Nixon and Negus, and framed by Strinati's observation that the cultural and the political have melded (1992, pp. 2–3). But, if journalists are 'cultural intermediaries', do they demonstrate that degree of independence from corporate goals which Bourdieu's vision of the 'cultural intermediary' indicates? The following section suggests not.

THE AUTONOMY AND STATUS OF JOURNALISTS

'News is whatever the media tell us is news', wrote Halloran *et al.* (1970, p. 313) and, as Schlesinger (1987, p. 87) points out, its 'production is far from chaotic ... its organizational rationale is to aim at control and prediction'. Notwithstanding the practice in some quarters of destructuring the capitalist enterprise into flexibly specialized semi-autonomous production units, staffed by flexibly specialized semi-autonomous workers (Piore and Sabel 1984; Atkinson 1984), the pattern of change in the media has been towards mergers, production rationalization and mass manufacturing. To the extent that there has been flexible specialization in media production, it has been within the controlling framework of large and growing corporations. The independent programme production sector of British television, for example, is significantly dependent upon and directed by the broadcasting commissioners. Moreover, this element of flexible specialization does not much affect those journalists who work to the time-sensitive production of daily news, for which independent production companies are ill-suited and broadcasters still assume responsibility. But it can affect journalists working on more analytical, research-driven documentaries. However, the majority of British journalists do not currently exist as scattered and temporary workers. It is true that there are freelancers, selling copy to whichever news organization will buy it, and there are 'stringers', paid a retainer to supply locally-gathered stories and information on a regular basis to one news organization which is yet not the employer. But at present, the majority of journalists remain as permanent employees of large organizations. This is partly to do with the idiosyncratic knowledge which the competent journalist will build up around his or her patch, partly to do with corporate concerns to protect copyright, and partly to do with an organizational need to keep control over fast-paced production schedules. In these employment patterns there is little to suggest that the autonomy of journalists has grown, or their occupational status improved.

In corporate hands, organizational rationale includes also the goal of cost-efficiency in the deployment of journalist labour power. Newsgathering organizations have long adopted the practice of placing journalists on 'beats' (for example courts, council meetings, hospitals) where matters of public interest can be expected to materialize regularly (Tunstall 1971; Ericson *et al.* 1989). But where the expense of maintaining a 'beat' journalist is unacceptable, news manufacturers typically seek to pool their resources. This has been the case particularly in foreign affairs, where global news agencies emerged in the 19th century to provide coverage, in raw data or in copy form, to whoever would purchase it (Boyd-Barrett and Rantanen 1998, p. 19; Wallis and Baran 1990, pp. 55 onwards). But the global news agencies have their domestic equivalents, with consequences for staffing in newsrooms elsewhere.

One of the oldest domestic news agencies is the British Press Association (PA). Emerging with the spread of the provincial press, the PA was founded in the 1850s initially to provide copy of national and international news to the provincial press but subsequently also to the national press. Nowadays it employs around 1200 people, the majority being journalists, to produce news copy for sale to 'every national and regional daily newspaper, broadcasters, online publishers and a wide range of commercial organisations'. It also provides 'a wide range of business-to-business services to media, government and commercial organisations. These include weather reporting, audio and video services, TV and event listing guides, contract publishing and response and fulfilment services' (PA recruitment leaflet 2001).

For efficiency reasons and because it is servicing so many customers on the basis of different versions of the same raw data, the PA discriminates organizationally between newsgathering operations and news processing operations. For the former, the PA employs only graduate-trained journalists, some of whom will undergo further company training. For the latter, who constitute more than 50 per cent of the PA's editorial staff, a journalism training is an advantage but is not regarded as essential. What is essential is a first-class grasp of English, for these are the 'production journalists' whose task is to take the raw data and convert it into so many news products for so many different paying clients. The speed of their production is anchored in the standardization of house styles (one per client) to which the writer must conform, and the number of pieces of copy to be produced in a given time frame. The processes of news production are thus both standardized and routinized. Moreover, while the newsgathering journalists can expect a degree of geographic mobility, the news production journalists cannot: they are tied to their computer terminals. Thus in this economically efficient deployment of journalist labour is born a status division between those who gather news and those who process news, the latter being what Bromley refers to as 'technicians-with-words' (1997, p. 346).

That the Press Association has found sufficient numbers of paying clients is largely to do with the search for cost savings among other news media. In the provincial press for example, the numbers of journalists employed to work at local and regional levels have dropped considerably on a per title basis. Franklin and Murphy (1998) chart the consequences in terms of an increasing reliance by the provincial press on ready-made copy from elsewhere. That copy comes either from news agencies at a cost, or from centralized production units of the provincial chain, or it comes freely from organizations and individuals who have developed their own journalism capacities and who have an interest in securing publication. Canadian press journalists report with dismay on the same experience: for them what has been lost is any capacity to integrate with and speak for local communities.

Stripping out journalists from newsrooms, moreover, was preceded by the stripping out of technical staff, which has meant that journalists nowadays have to be technically competent in the use of computer-based and digital technologies of production. They may even be required to develop multi-platform authoring skills such that they can support online versions of their news title simultaneously with its paper version. To that extent, they confirm the picture painted by such as Atkinson (1984) of workers in the new forms of capitalist enterprise being more functionally flexible than their predecessors. But they are functionally flexible within a division of labour which distinguishes between news gatherers and news processors, the 'journalism' of the latter being anchored in standardization, routinization, centralization and geographical immobility. This is not, in other words, the picture painted by Piore and Sabel (1984) of contemporary capitalism as a linked series of dispersed semi-autonomous production units.

The same processes of production rationalization are now underway in British radio and television. In autumn 2002, the industry regulator for commercial radio, the Radio Authority, took submissions on a proposal from the industry to allow the creation of 'regional news hubs'. The industry's argument was that it was no longer economically efficient to maintain a capacity for news production at each local radio station, and that there should instead be regional 'news hubs', or news teams, from which local stations could draw ready-made audio. At the same time, the Press Association initiated audio training for its journalists with the goal of selling audio copy to the commercial radio sector. More recently, the BBC and the Press Association announced a 'news partnership', the details of which are not, at the time of writing, known. In Canada, the 2001 purchase of Southam newspaper titles by the Aspers television family is a further example of the search for synergies in news production.

These more centralized modes of news production can lead to blandness and superficiality in news treatments. That is, to maximize sales and/or audience potential, centralized news production units are likely to construct event-driven news agenda, in which facts rather than analysis or opinion are prioritized. Moreover, acceptability to audiences remains crucial. Halloran *et al.* (1970, p. 314) comment that news 'material is so frequently produced with acceptability in mind, it is almost as though there was a silent conspiracy to present and receive the easy, the simple and the unambiguous'. Similarly, news publishers seeking to maximize audience appeal will probably increase the proportion of stories which are light, lifestyle or entertainment-oriented in relation to coverage of the serious and weighty. Thus it may be reasonable to draw a parallel between the production of news for mass consumption and the production of hamburgers for McDonalds: the goal in each instance is to produce an easily palatable, tasty bite of maximum consumer appeal. Moreover, it will be produced from a smaller number of journalists working to more pressurized production schedules, with a division of labour which locates news gatherers separately from news processors, and puts all under the command of editorial executives whose tasks are not merely to judge the news agenda of the moment but to seek and secure additional client-purchasers.

Centralized and increasingly pressurized news production arrangements push in the same direction, of routinization and standardization. Nick Jones (1995, p. 127) describes contemporary journalism as 'production line journalism'. He is referring to the requirements on broadcast journalists to turn out material to ever earlier and more frequent deadlines or, for 24-hour rolling news, constantly. He is referring to the requirements to produce materials in the same working time for more than one outlet, more than one medium or more than one programme. Such production pressures contribute to the cutting of corners in standards, such as ensuring that each piece of raw data has at least two sources of verification (see also Katz 1992; MacGregor 1997, pp. 177 and following; Ursell 2003) and they result in a focus on that which is immediate and simple over that which is enduring and complex (Cottle 1999, p. 281).

These developments have led some longer-serving journalists to express concerns: for example, Martin Wainwright, northern correspondent of *The Guardian*, commented, 'There's been tremendous damage done ... modern journalism is a shallow trade, it's a very superficial acitivity'; and Gaby Rado, foreign correspondent at Channel 4, described himself as 'worried about the future of serious journalism ... Even Channel 4 News is under pressure to shorten stories, cover the less difficult, be more like the big American news bureaus'. Evidence from the United States of America suggests that employment and work changes have contributed to lower journalist job satisfaction and morale (Weaver and Wilhoit 1992, pp. 10–11; Kurtz 1995), but the evidence from Britain (Delano and Henningham 1996, p. 18) is that morale is less affected. They suggest (pp. 17–18) that this has something to do with the 'division of British journalism into distinct, and increasingly discrete, tabloid and broadsheet cultures with quite different expectations'.

For trainee journalists, the immediate problem is one of inadequate pay – starting salaries are minimal, the lowest in 2003 under £9000 (Dear 2003). But the broader news agenda of today's media is typically seen as a positive development, enabling a personal interest in sports, music, fashion and/or show business to be pursued in the context of a junior reporter's role. Young journalists these days are invariably graduate-trained, or even postgraduate, and ideas about the Fourth Estate and public service will have been studied. A survey (Hanna, Sanders and Ball 2002/3) among students at the commencement of their vocational journalism training at eight UK institutions revealed that 84 per cent of (283) undergraduates and 87 per cent of (341) postgraduates upheld the value of getting information to the public quickly; 63 per cent (undergraduates) and 77 per cent (postgraduates) said the news media should investigate the claims and statements made by government; 51 per cent (undergraduates) and 67 per cent (postgraduates) said it was the news media responsibility to provide analysis and interpretation of complex problems; and 54 per cent (undergraduates) and 42 per cent (postgraduates) felt the news media should give ordinary people a chance to express their views on public affairs. The identity of journalists as offering a public service reflecting on government still seems secure. The same survey also revealed that the notion of public service did not though, for the majority, translate into the idea of journalists as political advocates. Only 10 per cent of the undergraduates and 15 per cent of the postgraduates felt that an extremely important task of the news media was to influence public opinion, while only 11 per cent of the undergraduates and 8 per cent of the postgraduates felt the media should set the political agenda. The contemporary professional identity of British journalists seems thus to maintain Fourth Estate and public service values but not to the point of political advocacy. Given the extent to which Britain's national daily press adopt explicit political positions, this novitiate opinion is perhaps to be understood by reference to their current situation in higher education training, and their immediate career prospects in the politically more neutral provincial press or in public service broadcasting. Hanna, Sanders and Ball will be canvassing these same cohorts of students at the culmination of their studies, at which point comparisons which throw light on the effects of journalism training will become possible. The researchers anticipate that preliminary findings will become available in 2004.

Finally, there is one aspect of relatively recent developments in journalism which can act as a magnet to some recruits. This is the prospect of becoming a 'star'. Star news presenters and reporters can expect good salaries (for example £150 000 for a provincial TV anchor) as well as public recognition. The prospect of fame and fortune obscures for many its implication for identity formation: that is, the aspiring individual must cultivate a 'persona' which works sufficiently well with audiences that media employers want to buy it. It can be proposed that this is an instance of Castells's 'project identity' as forged within a highly competitive, media environment. That is, it is a market-led identity. As such it may inflict a price on journalists as individuals simultaneously with raising concerns for standards of journalism. Kate Adie, a BBC foreign correspondent, has recently complained, for example, that older women television reporters are being pushed to one side to make way for younger women, who are 'cute faces and cute bottoms and nothing else in between' (Adie 2002).

MOBILITY

The case has been made above that geographical mobility varies according to the 'type' of journalist, that is, news gathering journalists travel but news processors do not. Travelling journalists include foreign correspondents, those covering the present fashion for buying property abroad, holiday show journalists, sports journalists and business and political reporters. Their ranks are swollen by the few aspiring journalists who are appointed as editorial executives or who move sideways into politics and become influencers of governments (for example, Alistair Campbell, ex-Director of Communications to UK Prime Minister Blair). These few may be 'symbolic analysts' and 'networkers' in the sense of members of a decision-making élite as conceptualized by Reich or Castells. But they are a minority of the 60 000 journalists working in Britain, and they will probably contain an above average number of 'stars' who must subordinate their newsgathering activities to presentational demands. What of the majority?

Following Reich's analysis (1991), Angell highlights the significance of globalized capitalism for the division of labour. He postulates that 'We are entering a new élite cosmopolitan age' (1995, pp. 10–12), in which the élites will comprise mobile and independent knowledge workers whose services are indispensable and, importantly, cannot be undertaken by robots or be exported to other parts of the globe. All other types of employee, in other words, stand in perpetual insecurity because their services can be dispensed with at the will of globally operating corporations. How do journalists stand in relation to this analysis?

It is undoubtedly the case that news production is or is becoming absorbed into multi-media conglomerates, some of which are international and one of which is global (namely, Murdoch's News Corporation). Within these conglomerates, journalists are increasingly divided into three broad echelons – at the top are the few 'stars' and their travelling companions in the form of foreign and other specialist reporters; then there are newsgatherers moving at national and provincial levels; finally there are news processors who operate within centralized production units reworking raw data supplied from elsewhere. The range of topics now embraced under the general heading of 'news' is very broad, and includes much material which is not time-bound and which is of interest to audiences everywhere. It is not impossible to envisage a multinational or global media conglomerate shifting all news processing of that kind of material out of, say, Britain and into, say, Hong Kong, if the latter promises lower labour costs. Even some time-bound material, such as TV listings, film reviews or the weather can now notionally be produced in one country for another, given the speed and range of the telecommunications and electronic infrastructures. It would seem then that this third tier of production journalists are among the routine production workers who are, in Reich's and Angell's analysis, permanently disposable and at the bottom of the employment hierarchy.

However, as Angell further argues (1995, p. 11), global companies have a genuine dependency on certain workers in localized production units or other locally constituted companies. This reflects in part the global company's need for local expertise in interpreting consumer demand, political and economic activity, or social and cultural trends. In another part, it reflects the global company's needs to access home markets in its search for niche and mass consumption. One can accordingly suggest that for newsgathering journalists, for reporters and those production journalists who specialize in the interpretation of consumer demand, political and economic activity and social and cultural trends, and who facilitate the entrepreneurial and political management of domestic populations, there will be employment security and indeed some reasonable status. These are, it can be suggested, the 'cultural intermediaries' of the Nixon and Negus analyses or the 'support workers' of Reich's. They do not, however, demonstrate that degree of independence from the media corporations that might entitle them to be designated the 'cultural intermediaries' of Bourdieu's perspective.

SUMMARY AND CONCLUDING REFLECTIONS

The account above has charted the rise of the journalist occupation in the context of the institutionalization of the Fourth Estate, politically constructed as a 'free press'. The specification of journalist identity in that context has been here represented as 'legitimizing'. But, as journalists have experienced potentially de-legitimizing pressures from 'free press' proprietors or from politically appointed external appraisers, they have taken collective action to assert the professionalism of their occupation. That is, the terms of the legitimating identity have been adopted as terms of resistance; the legitimating identity has become the resistant identity.

However, since the late 20th century, the very terms of legitimization have become contested. This is in the context of the great expansion in different applications of journalism skills and personnel, accompanied by substantial re-organization of journalists' division of labour. The outcome, it is argued here, has been to create new hierarchies. At the top are journalists engaged to some extent in project identity formation, and enjoying some degree of autonomy, status and geographic mobility. At the bottom are production journalists, existing as insecure and disposable workers. Those in the middle are secure in the sense of being essential to the efficiency of the global political economy, but their autonomy, status and mobility is limited by their existence as corporate employees.

In terms of the conceptualizations of a new breed of information worker, journalists are not a new breed. But their occupation reveals remarkable internal differentiation such that, by looking at different types of journalist, we can readily describe some as 'symbolic analysts' and 'networkers', others as 'support workers', and yet others as 'day labourers'. In that respect, this empirical case study reveals the limits to some of the conceptualizations: it is clearly not enough to describe all information and networking workers as the new élite.

There is one closing reflection. The journalists considered above are already, or are in the process of becoming, employees of corporations. Insofar as they and the wider public are dissatisfied with corporate uses of journalism, there is motivation for the emergence of non-corporate journalism. The new technologies will facilitate that emergence. In the non-corporate domain is space for the pursuit and survival of the older legitimating identity of journalists. It remains possible therefore that they will contribute once again to the emergence of a new polity, not of the nation-state but one more suited to globalised relationships and systems. This may be their contribution to the independent and relatively autonomous 'cultural intermediaries' of Bourdieu's vision.

REFERENCES

Adie, K. (2002), *The Kindness of Strangers*, London: Headline.
Angell, A. (1995), 'Winners and Losers in the Information Age', *LSE Magazine*, **7** (1), pp. 10–12.
Atkinson, J. (1984), 'Manpower Strategies for Flexible Organisations', *Personnel Management*, August, pp. 28–31.
Barnett, S. and E. Seymour (1999), *A Shrinking Iceberg Travelling South: Changing Trends in British Television: A Case Study of Drama and Current Affairs*, London:

Campaign for Quality Television.
Beck, U. (1992), *Risk Society: Towards a New Modernity*, London: Sage.
Bourdieu, P. (1986), *Distinction: A Social Critique of the Judgment of Taste*, London: Routledge.
Bourdieu, P. (1998), *On Television and Journalism*, London: Pluto.
Boyd-Barrett, O. and T. Rantanen (eds) (1998), *The Globalisation of News*, London: Sage.
Bromley, M. (1997), 'The End of Journalism', in M. Bromley and T. O'Malley (eds), *A Journalism Reader*, London: Routledge.
Bromley, M. (ed.) (2001), *No News is Bad News: Radio, Television and the Public*, Harlow: Pearson Education.
Burns, T. (1977), *The BBC: Private World, Public Institution*, London: Macmillan.
Carlyle, T. (1840), *Heroes, Hero-Worship and the Heroic in History*, London: Chapman & Hall.
Castells, M. (1996), *The Rise of Network Society*, Oxford: Basil Blackwell.
Castells, M. (1997), *The Power of Identity*, Oxford: Blackwell.
Cottle, S. (1999), 'From BBC Newsroom to BBC Newscentre: On Changing Technology and Journalist Practices', *Convergence*, **5** (3), pp. 22–43.
Dahlgren, P. and C. Sparks (eds) (1991), *Communication and Citizenship: Journalism and the Public Sphere*, London: Routledge.
Dear, J. (2003), General Secretary of the National Union of Journalists, quoted in HoldtheFrontPage at http://www.holdthefrontpage.co.uk/behind/analysis/030911dear.shtml (accessed 1 April 2004).
Delano, A. and J. Henningham (1996), *The News Breed: British Journalists in the 1990s*, London: The London Institute.
Desbarats, P. (1996), *Guide to Canadian News Media*, 2nd edn, Toronto: Harcourt Brace.
Du Gay, P., J. Evans and P. Redman (2000), *Identity: A Reader*, London: Sage.
Ericson, R. V., P. M. Baranek and J. B. L. Chan (1989), *Negotiating Control: A Study of News Sources*, Milton Keynes: Open University.
Franklin, R. (1997), *Newszak and News Media*, London: St Martin's.
Franklin, R. and D. Murphy (1998), *Making the Local News: Local Journalism in Context*, London: Routledge.
Frost, C. (2000), *Media Ethics and Self Regulation*, Harlow: Longman.
Giddens, A. (1990), *The Consequences of Modernity*, Cambridge: Polity Press.
Giddens, A. (1991), *Modernity and Self-Identity*, Cambridge: Polity Press.
Habermas, J. (1974), 'The Public Sphere: An Encyclopaedia Article', *New German Critique*, **3**, pp. 49–55.
Habermas, J. (1984), *The Theory of Communicative Action, Vol. 1: Reason and the Rationalization of Society*, Cambridge: Polity Press.
Habermas, J. (1979), *Communication and the Evolution of Society*, London: Heinemann.
Halloran, J. D., P. Elliott and G. Murdock (1970), *Demonstrations and Communications*, Harmondsworth: Penguin.
Hanna, M., K. Sanders and A. Ball, Research in progress from 2002. Contact Mark Hanna, Department of Journalism Studies, University of Sheffield for further details.
Harcup, T. (2001), The Ethics of Journalism: A Trade Union Issue?, *Faculty Research Paper*, March, Leeds: Trinity and All Saints College.
Harcup, T. (2002), 'Journalists and Ethics: The Quest for a Collective Voice', *Journalism Studies*, **3** (1), pp. 101–14.

IMS (1989), *Skill Search: TV, Film and Video Employment Patterns and Training*, London: Institute of Manpower Studies.
Johnson, T. (1972), *Professions and Power*, London: Macmillan.
Jones, N. (1995), *Soundbites and Spin Doctors*, London: Indigo.
Journalism Training Forum (2002), *Journalists at Work: Their Views on Training, Recruitment and Conditions*, London: NTO/Skillset, July.
Katz, E. (1992), 'The End of Journalism: Notes on Watching the War', *Journal of Communication*, **42** (3), pp. 5–13.
Kurtz, H. (1995), 'Frightening News for Papers', *International Herald Tribune*, 1st November, pp. 13–17.
Lash, S. and J. Urry (1994), *Economies of Signs and Space*, London: Sage.
Lyotard, J.-F. (1984), *The Postmodern Condition: A Report on Knowledge*, Manchester: Manchester University Press.
MacGregor, B. (1997), *Live, Direct and Biased: Making TV News in the Satellite Age*, London: Arnold.
Mansfield, F. J. (1943), *Gentlemen, the Press!*, London: W. H. Allen.
Morley, D. (2000), *Home Territories: Media, Mobility and Identity*, London: Routledge.
Negus, K. (1997), 'The Production of Culture', in Paul du Gay (ed.), *Production of Culture/Cultures of Production*, London: Sage, pp. 67–118.
Newspaper Society (1997), *Reaching the Regions*, London: The Newspaper Society.
Nixon, S. (1997), 'Circulating Culture', in Paul du Gay (ed.), *Production of Culture/Cultures of Production*, London: Sage, pp. 177–234.
O'Malley, T. and C. Soley (2000), *Regulating the Press*, London: Pluto.
Paine, T. (1791), *The Rights of Man*, Dover Publications, reprinted 1999.
Piore, M. and C. Sabel (1984), *The Second Industrial Divide*, New York: Basic Books.
Reich, R. B. (1991), *The Work of Nations*, New York: Knopf.
Robertson, G. (1983), *People Against the Press: An Enquiry into the Press Council*, London: Quartet.
Rose, N. (1998), *Inventing Our Selves: Psychology, Power and Personhood*, Cambridge: Cambridge University Press.
Rose, N. (1999), *Powers of Freedom: Reframing Political Thought*, Cambridge: Cambridge University Press.
Schlesinger, P. (1987), *Putting 'Reality' Together*, London, New York: Methuen.
Stephenson, H. (1998), 'Tickle the Punter: Consumerism Rules', in H. Stephenson and M. Bromley (eds), *Sex, Lies and Democracy: The Press and the Public*, London: Longman, pp. 13–24.
Stephenson, H. and Bromley, M. (eds) (1998), *Sex, Lies and Democracy: The Press and the Public*, London: Longman.
Stokes, J. and A. Reading (eds) (1999), *The Media in Britain: Current Debates and Developments*, Basingstoke: Palgrave.
Strinati, D. (1992), 'Postmodernism and Popular Culture', *Sociology Review*, April, pp. 2–7.
Tulloch, J. (1998), 'Managing the Press in a Medium-Sized European Power', in H. Stephenson and M. Bromley (eds), *Sex, Lies and Democracy: The Press and the Public*, London: Longman.
Tunstall, J. (1971), *Journalists at Work*, London: Constable.
Ursell, G. (2003), 'Creating Value and Valuing Creation in Contemporary UK Television: Or "Dumbing Down" the Workforce', *Journalism Studies*, **4** (1), pp. 31–46.

Wallis R. and S. Baran (1990), *The Known World of Broadcast News: International News and the Electronic Media*, London: Routledge.

Weaver, D. and G. C. Wilhoit (1992), *The American Journalist in the 1990s*, Arlington VA: The Freedom Forum.

3. The networking arena
Torben Elgaard Jensen

'We offer a place to grow both your business and yourself'. This inviting statement appears on the homepage of the company that will be studied in the present chapter. The company, called United Spaces, is an office hotel located in Stockholm and in Copenhagen. Its basic service is to provide a shared office space for small innovative firms. But space is merely one element; United Spaces calls itself a network office, and it actively works to create an environment and a culture in which 'networking' will flourish and grow. This ambition is clearly visible in the physical layout of the company. In Copenhagen, United Spaces is located on the ground floor of a new office building on the harbour front. One large room called the networking arena dominates the ground floor. This is an open office space with sixty workstations arranged in small groups. A mobile Intranet is installed, which allows the members to access the Internet and the local printer from their laptops regardless of their position in the room. The two managers encourage the members of United Spaces to place themselves and their laptops at a new workstation every day. Through this mingling, they argue, every member will 'automatically' generate a broad array of contacts. United Spaces is thus trying to localize and enhance a particular form of practice, which is often referred to as networking. As indicated by the opening quotation, this practice is believed to grow businesses as well as selves. The aim of this chapter is to investigate how the world is ordered at United Spaces, and how identities are performed as an integral part of this ordering.

As a form of organization, United Spaces might broadly be labelled as a networking environment; it is a location where individuals and smaller enterprises mingle and combine products and knowledge in innovative ways. In recent years, Silicon Valley is undoubtedly the single most famous case of a network environment; a case that requires no further introduction. But the stimulation of flexible and lateral *ad hoc* connections seems to take place on a wider scale, which is evidenced by a number of fashionable reorganization strategies:

- Internal markets are established within companies in order to stimulate

networking and knowledge sharing between people and organizational units.
- Radical outsourcing is employed as a strategy to turn the company into a flexible player in a network of businesses.
- 'Learning organizations' are designed to make every employee an acting and thinking networker rather than a pawn awaiting orders from above.

Whether successful or not, all of these strategies may be seen as attempts to create network environments.

Although it seems likely that network environments are on the rise, the strategy of the present chapter is not to extrapolate this observation into grand speculation about the rise of a network society (compare Castells 2001). The reason for not doing this is quite simple. If we assume from the beginning that network environments are the first signs of a radically different future, then we limit our scope of interest to the big differences; we are tempted to believe that the identity of network-people is entirely different from the identity of, say, bureaucrats, and therefore a study of a network environment must be a search for the exotic secrets of the network-tribe.[1] With this line of thinking, the possible continuities and more subtle differences between network environments and other forms of work are neglected.

The problem suggested is not merely that Castells and others[2] tend to follow the hype about networks. The real problem is that network environments are treated as some kind of solution, which can be taken as the premise for further speculation. In this way, network environments themselves are not made an object of empirical sociological analysis. The present chapter follows an analytical strategy that works in the opposite direction. It analyses practice, that is the events, actions, practical circumstances, ordering of work, and identity that constitute United Spaces. In this way, the networking environment is treated as a question rather than an answer (compare Suchman 1987; Star 1992). This alternative approach does not pretend to be neutral; it imports its own assumptions and consequences. The most significant one may be that the analytical boundary between identity and organization is blurred. When practice is made the analytical focus, nouns such as identity and organization are transformed into verbs such as identifying and organizing (Law 1994). This process recursively produces interdependent effects such as work being organized, and particular shapes of people being recognized and recognizable (Lave and Wenger 1991). So just as United Spaces claims to be a place to grow both your business and yourself, the analysis of practice claims to be a strategy for studying both organizing and identifying.

What then, are the possible ways in which identity or identifying is produced at United Spaces? It goes without saying that the answer to this question depends on what exactly is meant by identity. In the following, I shall indicate three broad positions on identity in the sociological literature, relating to personal histories, belonging and subjectification. I shall use these well-established positions in two ways. In the following section, I shall use them to generate questions for the case study of United Spaces. Later, at the end of this chapter, I shall anchor the analysis by discussing how the practice at United Spaces compares with the analyses of identity based on these three positions.

THEORIZING IDENTITY

The most common way to conceptualize identity is to focus on personal histories. The project of identity is then a project of integrating a stream of life events into a relatively coherent formation. On the supportive side, a number of processes may be listed, such as solving conflicts, making friends, gradual improvement through learning, and the accumulation of savings in the broadest sense of the word. On the obstructive side, all sorts of dramatic changes, insecurities, losses and conflicts, may threaten the coherent formation of identity.

Richard Sennett (1998) gives a clear example of this view of identity. He has recently made the argument that character is corroded in the 'new economy'. This corrosion, he argues, is linked to the fact that accumulation is no longer possible. In earlier times, it was possible to get a steady, although perhaps relatively boring job. Based on this job, it was possible to provide for a family and little by little it would be possible to accumulate savings for old age. The repetitiveness of the job was directly linked to security, predictability and savings. For this reason, hard and steady work earned respect from family and friends. Sennett claims that accumulation, and hence a stable character, is no longer possible. Constant changes of jobs, career paths and physical locations destroy the possibility of accumulation. Taking these arguments to the case of United Spaces, one might address the issue of identity by examining the possibilities (or impossibilities) of accumulation.

A second conceptualization links identity to belonging. To develop identity is to become enculturated into social worlds (Strauss 1978) or cultural subgroups that share particular customs, practices, values, linguistic codes, and so on. Identity is thus about connecting and identifying with others. It is about finding one's place, and it is about becoming a constitutive part of a social formation larger than oneself. The literature on the so-called communities of practice may be cited as an example of this view of identity (Lave and Wenger 1991; Brown and Duguid 1991; Wenger 1998). This literature examines social learning as a dual process that, over an extended period of time, transforms the newcoming member and the community itself.

Taking this perspective to the case of United Spaces, one might ask how identity and identifying is managed in a setting where the daily mixing of subgroups seems to be the order of the day.

Third and finally, I shall mention conceptualizations of identity inspired by Foucault. Identity in this view is about subjectification. Subjects are made through intellectual and practical techniques, in the form of rationalized schemes that configure and enable particular forms of subjectivity and practice. Rather than assuming a trans-historical subject, Foucauldians' claim is that the ontology of the subject is historical. For this reason the analysis of subjectivity – or identity – would require close attention to the various practical ways in which people get made at a given time: How are people rendered problematic? What are the systems of judgement or evaluation? What are the technical means of leading subjects in desired directions? Who is accorded the capacity and authority to speak truthfully about the nature of human beings and their problems? What forms of ideals or exemplars are working upon persons? (Rose 1996, pp. 313–14).

A number of studies of subjectification in working life take direct inspiration from Foucault's analysis of the panopticon principle in *Discipline and Punish* (Foucault 1975/1991). Foucault emphasizes the role of particular forms of visibility in the process of subjectification. He argues that the omnipresent threat of surveillance (dramatically illustrated by Bentham's ideal prison) leads to self-monitoring, which then turns the self into a prison. Along the same lines, critical analyses have been made of the subjectification practices brought about by accounting systems and performance measurement (Townley 1996), and by Total Quality Management (Sewell and Wilkinson 1992; Knights and McCabe 2000). Drawing on this analytical perspective, one might study the construction of identity at United Spaces by attending to the particular kinds of visibility that are created. This might include architectural techniques such as the open office space plan, and normative-governmental features such as the rule of changing tables every day.

With this listing of possible lines of questions about identity (personal history, belonging, subjectification), it is time to turn to the empirical exploration of how identity is performed in a networking environment. Rather than pursuing one particular theoretical perspective on identity, I shall attempt to build a broad account of the processes of relating, being and identifying at United Spaces. On the basis of this account of practice, I shall return to the various perspectives on identity at the end of this chapter. To begin, I shall work my way into the case study by means of the question that inspired and haunted me during a month of fieldwork. Everybody at United Spaces seemed to talk about networking. Everybody seemed to do networking. The whole place seemed to be about networking. But what *is* networking in practice?

VERSIONS OF NETWORKING

To investigate what networking is and how it is done at United Spaces one must find a suitable starting point: a segment of practice, a first encounter. A fairly standard way to encounter an unknown company is to visit its homepage. It would be quite misleading to regard a homepage as a detached description of a company. A homepage *does* things: it makes promises to the reader, it raises expectations, it creates trustworthiness, and it may even take your money. In short, the homepage helps make the company what it is. An analytical separation of text versus action, or signifier versus signified makes little sense in the case of homepages. A homepage is part of the action, and therefore a potentially interesting place to study the workings of a company (compare Law 2002, ch. 8).[3] The homepage of United Spaces depicts the company through a texture of images and text: pictures of members and the building; logos and graphics in bright colours; descriptions of the business concept, the culture of United Spaces and its organizational set-up; information about the membership fee and the list of services provided; and links to the homepages of all member companies.

As a first step in investigating what network is, I used the built-in search engine to find occurrences of the word 'network'. It is unsurprising that 'network' and its derivatives 'networked' and 'networking' turned up frequently (24 hits). However, it is more surprising to find that the term seems to cover a number of different versions of network. The types of nodes that make up the network differ; the types of relations between these nodes differ; and the effects of these nodes and relations differ. Taking inspiration from the work of Annemarie Mol and John Laws on social topology (Mol and Law 1994),[4] I have identified three different ideal types or versions of network: network-as-a-club, network-as-a-chain, and network-as-acquaintances.

Network-as-a-club

In a number of places on the homepage, United Spaces is depicted as a club. People using United Spaces are referred to as members, which they are by virtue of paying a monthly membership fee. This grants them access to the building at any time and permission to use various pieces of office equipment and facilities. On a completely practical level, the boundary between members and non-members is managed through artefacts such as key cards, access codes and mobile Intranet connections. But the homepage suggests that practical means of access is only one dimension of membership. Members also share certain values:

> At United Spaces collaboration and partnership are keywords, which is acknowledged by everyone.

The common values, as well as some required characteristics, are spelled out in detail in the following statement aimed at potential members:

> Why should I become a Member? Because you believe that the best concepts are created through a continuous exchange of ideas with others and that a well-organised network is the best way to capitalise on those ideas. And you are an open-minded individual who seeks personal development and believes that by giving you gain. In addition you value generosity, openness, curiosity, responsibility, competence, collaboration, respect and trust.

The version of network suggested is defined by the similarities of the members. Despite the differences that they might have, they all acknowledge certain keywords and share a number of beliefs. New members, it appears, must accept this as well. The essential similarity among the members, combined with the boundedness of the club, suggests a particular distribution of sameness and difference. What is inside the boundaries, and hence close, is similar. What is outside the boundaries, and hence distant, is different (compare Mol and Law 1994, p. 647). The club version of network then goes together with the idea that reality is composed of patches or regions which do not overlap and which are mutually exclusive. United Spaces is a unique place with its own culture; the company next door is something entirely different.

Network-as-a-chain

Although the members seem to be the focal point of United Spaces, as well as the chief source of income, there are other important actors.

> Partners and Network
> United Spaces can be viewed upon as a high-end network of people and companies – a marketplace for ideas, services and products. A marketplace cannot work without services and products, which are why we establish partnerships with the right companies – to improve the value of the United Spaces offer to the members. United Spaces extends the network beyond the networking arena, by establishing different types of partnerships. This is done to strengthen the service offer, and to give the members opportunities to benefit from relevant services.

Three different types of partners are then explained: strategic partners that work with United Spaces to develop the services offered to the members (for example Hewlett Packard, that has developed a mobile Intranet solution for United Spaces); service networks, which are local partners that offer services at special discount prices to the members (for example accounting); and supporting partners/ambassadors, which are corporations or individuals that help create new business opportunities for United Spaces.

The network with partners differs from the network-as-club on several counts. Partners are actors that are able to perform something that United Spaces or its members cannot do themselves. Difference rather than similarity is thus the criterion for inclusion. Moreover, this kind of network is based on a quite specific form of contact. The partnership relations are formed through negotiation, specification and formalization of services and prices. Where members mingle informally, partners relate in relatively specific and formalized ways. This network-as-chain is thus a network that depends on stabilized functional relations among actors of different kinds. The functional relations, rather than a shared boundary, are what hold this version of network together. The network-as-a-chain is thus a value chain, a linkage of functionally differentiated actors that adds to the value of what is being produced at United Spaces.

Network-as-acquaintances

The main image conveyed by the homepage is that United Spaces is a distinguished club with a carefully chosen set of external partners. However, a third version of network is also indicated. On a subpage listing what is required of an ambassador, you find the following lines:

- Look out for opportunities – for partner and establishment

- Spread the word of United Spaces to relevant policymakers and key people.

These lines seem to indicate that, in addition to members and partners, there is a version of network that consists of acquaintances of various sorts. On several occasions, I have heard members of United Spaces make a similar suggestion by saying that at United Spaces 'there is always someone who knows someone'.

The network of acquaintances is productively undefined in several senses. It is unclear what role an acquaintance might come to play: buyer, seller, intermediary, informer or something else? It is also unclear where an interesting acquaintance might appear. Who precisely is it that knows someone? The network-as-acquaintances is like the rhizome depicted by Deleuze and Guattari (1987); it grows from everywhere and in all directions; it may connect any point to any other point; it has no beginning or end; it is an open map. The ideal type, which I call acquaintance network, is thus in a constant stage of becoming, and this makes it a network beyond the well-defined links between partners and beyond the well-defined location of a club.

Table 3.1 Three versions of network

	Club	**Chain**	**Acquaintances**
Nodes	similar	different	undefined
Relations	informal	formalized	undefined
Effects	bounded region	functional relations	rhizome

ESTABLISHED DISORDER

Let us ask the question again: What is networking in practice? In popular accounts of the so-called network society, networking is simply about connecting everything with everything (Castells 2001; Kelly 1999). However, as we have realized from a small set of empirical specifics gathered from the homepage of United Spaces, things are more complicated than that. There are different ways of making networks, and different versions. It is also clear that networking is not merely about increasing the number of connections. Each of the versions of network implies that certain kinds of connections are discouraged. In the club version, non-members are not granted access. In the chain version, actors who resemble yourself are useless. In the acquaintance version, people whom you known – directly or indirectly – are always preferred to strangers. So what is at stake in the building of networks at United Spaces is precisely not continual expansion, unlimited growth, or a frontier that can always be pushed further West. On the contrary, networking is about the making or re-making of relations in a space that is already filled with various versions of network.

The notion of a filled space has recently[5] been taken up by Zygmunt Bauman. He addresses the question of universal human ethics by going back to a text[6] written by Immanuel Kant in 1784. In this text, Kant argues that our essential humanity is linked to the fact that we live on a globe. This means that every time we move away from someone, we also move closer. For this reason, Kant argues, hospitality is not merely an important ethic, but the fundamental human ethic. Kant's text, Bauman explains, has not been taken seriously over the past 200 years, because it has been possible to pretend that the planet was not full. It was believed that it is always possible to find new virgin lands beyond the boundaries and the problems of the old world. In fact, the key strategy of modernity has been to export waste (physical, cultural and human) that did not fit the orders that modernism was trying to establish. The globe outside western civilisation was always there to receive. In reality, of course, there have never been any virgin lands; there were merely weaker countries that were treated as virgin lands by stronger countries. But Bauman argues that the modern era has come to an end. He takes the so-called immigration problem and the 9/11 attacks as clear signs that the world cannot be separated into secure and insecure zones. We can no longer pretend that the world is in the process of being filled. We are back to Kant's challenge to live together on a full planet.

The imagery of Kant and Bauman is sharply at odds with the imagery informing the predominant notions of network society. These latter accounts are deeply engaged with the illusion of 'virgin lands'. They take the world to be largely empty, waiting to be filled up with networks. People, places, artefacts are merely waiting to get connected (for example Kelly 1999). However, as I have argued above, network at United Spaces does not develop in a vacuum. Network comes in different and partially agonistic versions. What might be observed at United Spaces is not the filling up of an empty space, but rather an experiment in living together in a space that is already full.

Is United Spaces then really a place where Kant's and Bauman's challenges are met? On the one hand, there is no doubt that United Spaces is a communal experiment. 'We are building a new kind of global community', as they write in their advertising material. On the other hand, it is equally clear that United Spaces has no intention of including everyone indiscriminately. 'United Spaces can be thought of as a high-end community', as they write on their homepage. So there are certainly limits (including economic limits) to the idealism and the inclusiveness.

But United Spaces can, nonetheless, be thought of as a practical case of bringing the three above-mentioned versions of network together. At United Spaces we know that there are different versions of networks. We know that the versions operate differently, and we can therefore assume that there will be tensions or even conflicts between them. However, we can also assume that, by and large, these tensions do not reach a dramatic stage of conflict. If this were the case, United Spaces would have either dissolved or exploded by now. So at United Spaces there must be practical ways of living with the tension between different versions of network. It is these practices that I shall investigate in this chapter.

ANALYTICAL PROCEDURE

The investigation is based on empirical material gathered during one month of fieldwork. The two managers of United Spaces granted me access; they showed interest in my project and suggested that I became a member. I accepted this invitation and paid the membership fee for one month.

Through the month of February 2002, I arrived at United Spaces every morning with my laptop. I seated myself at different workstations. I

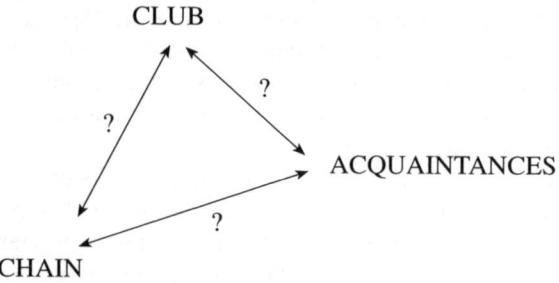

Figure 3.1   Analytical model

interviewed the two managers and a number of the members. I engaged in informal conversations over coffee or lunch. I searched for meetings and events to observe. And I collected physical or electronic documents. The question that guided the data collection was a relatively open one. I focused on how relations were constructed in real-time: relations between members, or relations between members and other parties. This focus led to observations and stories about business, practical help, knowledge sharing, inspiration, irritation, friendship and many other issues.

As a means of moving from the pile of collected material to a systematic analysis, a heuristic simplification was made. Figure 3.1 transforms the tri-fold tension between three versions of network into a list of dual tensions: (1) chain versus club, (2) club versus acquaintances, (3) chain versus acquaintances.

For each of these pairs, the material has been searched for stories that would elucidate the tension and the practical co-existence between the two versions of network. Evidently, this is an exploratory procedure that favours breadth over depth. It does not make an exhaustive analysis of all the ways tension is lived with at United Spaces. But it does capture at least some of the practical ways of living with tension between each of the possible configurations of the three different network versions.

Between Chain and Club

One can imagine various forms of tension between a club made of equals with no specific division of roles and a chain made of un-equals with a specific division of roles. At United Spaces, this tension is visible in situations that blend the mutual sharing of an office space with the potential forging of a buyer and seller relationship between the members.

> Allergic to Sales Talk
> Michael tells of a new member in United Spaces who made a very bad impression

on him. The new member was a lawyer, and at a joint meeting ('an arena meeting'), where he was introduced to the other members, he made a sales speech about all the different things that he could offer small start-up firms. Michael declares that he is 'allergic' to this kind of sales talk.

In this story, Michael clearly states that the arena meetings should not be turned into occasions for sale. Michael's 'allergy' suggests that a foreign body has entered a space where it does not belong. The foreign body is the forging of buyer and seller relationships, the construction of a functional division of roles – that is the chain version of network. This is at odds with the arena meeting, which constitutes a time-space where the common concerns of the members can be addressed. The focus in the arena meeting is, or should be, the construction of a membership 'we': collective agreements and mutual adjustments of values and expectations. The arena meeting is an occasion to perform the club version of network, to produce similarity – not to buy and sell. But, at other times, on other occasions, it seems to be the chain version of network that expels its others:

Shredding
Charlotte is standing in the photocopy room. She is doing the bothersome job of shredding a large pile of papers. A person from another United Spaces company is using the photocopier. She asks Charlotte if it is really necessary to shred all those papers. Charlotte replies that the papers come from one of their clients – and anything coming from a client must be treated confidentially.

In this event, the chain and the club versions of network are once again held apart. Through the act of shredding, Charlotte destroys information from her client-relation in order to prevent its diffusion into the shared office space. So in this case, the network-as-chain and the confidentiality that goes with it, crucially depend on practices that prevent it from being mixed with the club version of network. However, there are also instances where the club and the commercial chains are actively brought together.

Free Agent Game
The consulting firm Agency Games developed a game called 'free agent'. In this game a number of players (for example 30) are given cards which indicate particular professions, skills and idea. The players are placed on an open floor. When the game begins, they are supposed to walk around and 'network', that is to find other players with supplementary skills and ideas, pool the resources, go to 'the bank', and cash in. The game exposes certain more-or-less fortunate network behaviours, such as making yourself visible, clinging on to a particular idea, focusing on fairness rather than speed. Agency Games invited the other members in United Spaces to play this game, among these John from another consulting firm. John was very impressed with the game, and later he invited Agency Games to be a subcontractor on one of his projects.

Rent-a-webmaster
Chris and Anne chat in the smoking room. Chris tells about an idea for a novel service product; he wants to update other companies' web pages. He will then be a Webmaster on a rental basis. Anne, who is a professional secretary, suggests that he includes proof reading as a part of the package. This quickly develops into an idea for a joint enterprise. Chris will deliver the content management system; Anne and her business partner will edit the new texts that the client company wants to put on the net.

Both of these stories begin with one company making itself visible to others. Agency Games invites the United Spaces members to participate in a game, which they direct. Chris explains a business idea which he has been thinking about. The construction of this visibility depends on several of the club-like aspects of United Spaces: proximity – the other members are physically there, so they can be showed something; and familiarity – the other members are a relatively known and trusted audience, which is not expected to steal customers or ideas. Following the visibility event, the other company returns a specific suggestion: why not make our service a part of your package? Or why not make your service a part of our package? And, finally this suggestion is accepted, which leads to the formation of a specific division of roles, and hence a chain-like network between the two companies. The transition from the club version to the chain version of network is complete.

How exactly is the tension between chain and club lived with in these two stories? Let us call the first company the sender and the second one the receiver. In the story about the 'crude' sales speech, one could say that the sender tries to define the role of the receiver. The lawyer expects himself to be the seller and he expects the other members to buy his specific products. He suggests a simple commercial exchange, *quid pro quo*. This is different in the two last stories. In these, the sender merely gives something of himself away, his ideas or his products. He does not define a specific role for the receiver, and the receiver is by no means obliged to pay. In spite of this, the receiver does in fact pay; he offers to construct a relationship that is valuable to the sender. But – and this is important – the return offered by the receiver is a suggestion that implies a specific division of roles. This means that the receiver is lowered and elevated at the same time; he plays the subordinate role of paying back and he plays the superordinate role of defining the division of roles. So a complicated balancing act emerges: the sender gives freely – and yet he is paid. The receiver acknowledges a debt – and yet he gets the upper hand in defining the relationship. Who is in charge? Is it the sender who cashes in, or is it the receiver who defines the relationship? This is undecided and therefore reconcilable with the club version of networking, where the members are essentially equals. Are the roles divided? Clearly so. A specific series of exchanges is defined. The output of one company becomes the input of another. The chain version of networking is in place.

So the specific sequence of events (visibility without demand, followed by a return in the form of a specific offer) makes it possible to live with two versions of networking at the same time. One can of course only speculate on how versions of networking will be worked together or held apart in the future exchanges between the two companies.

Between Club and Acquaintances

What might be the relation between network in the form of a swarm of acquaintances and network in the form of a selected and circumscribed group of club members? The club and the acquaintance version of network are related in the following story that describes some of the work that went into the construction of United Spaces in Copenhagen:

> Establishing United Spaces in Copenhagen
> Allison works in a consulting firm that is now a regular member of United Spaces. About two years ago this consulting firm was hired as the local partner of the Swedish consortium that wanted to establish a department of United Spaces in Copenhagen, similar to the one set up in Stockholm. One of the tasks was to do the 'network marketing' necessary to establish 'the cultural basis' of United Spaces in Copenhagen.
> A key task was to find a group of core members. The consulting firm did a marketing survey that gathered information about who would be interested in joining United Spaces what kinds of events and services they would want and which other companies they would prefer to see as members. However, this survey was not primarily intended to gather information. It was just as much to get the word about United Spaces out. The consulting firm deliberately surveyed companies that would be useful ambassadors for the concept, although some of these companies were very unlikely to become members of United Spaces. In this and several other ways, the consulting firm made sure that the message was spread in a wide range of environments.

In this story there is no tension, but rather a productive relationship between the club and the acquaintance version of network. The United Spaces consortium hires the consulting firm because their local swarm of acquaintances is useful to spread the word and to find suitable core members. Moreover, with the marketing survey, the consulting firm is making additional acquaintances and 'feeding' them with information that they might pass on to their acquaintances. All of this is instrumental in finding the right people to include in the 'club'.

A positive correlation is sketched here. The more acquaintances, the more 'network marketing' of United Spaces, the greater the chance to attract a highly select group of companies that would form a well-functioning club. Along with this correlation one might imagine a particular sequence. First came a rather loose network of acquaintances; later came a close-knit club. This does seem to be the case. The club is derived from acquaintances. But it would be wrong to assume that the network-as-acquaintances is replaced or pushed aside by the club.

Traffic
On a normal day, the office building of United Spaces looks more like a train station than a board meeting. Phone conversations, e-mails and SMS messages constantly pour in and out of the building. There is a steady flow of guests, friends, family and business partners in the office. In spite of these visitors, the office space is rarely full. On most days a large portion of the members are working elsewhere – most likely at home or with business partners. But no one knows exactly.

All of this traffic in and out of the house suggests that network-as-acquaintance is not a phase that is over and done with. It seems rather that this version of network is growing in, through and around the circumscribed building of United Spaces as well as in, through and around a number of other places. Again, the relationship between club and acquaintances seems to be mutually reinforcing, rather than mutually excluding.

So is there any tension between acquaintances and the club? Yes, there is. The management of United Spaces has set itself the goal of creating a particular culture among the members. The officially announced focus of this culture is to share knowledge and ideas with people and companies that are different from you. This managerial goal centres on various efforts to focus and increase the interaction among the members.

Changing Positions
The most salient device for increasing member interaction is the interior design and office furniture of United Spaces. The central, largest room is an open office space referred to as 'the networking arena'. In this room, sixty workstations are distributed across the floor. A workstation consists of a relatively small table about the height of a bar table, with a suitable office chair. In front of the table, there is a transparent Plexiglas screen that covers the average person to the shoulders. So everybody is highly visible in the networking arena. Between the Plexiglas screen and the table there is a small lamp and sockets for electrical plugs and for a telephone line. Each workstation comes with a small roller cabinet, used for personal papers and belongings. Most of the workstations are placed in small groups with the workstations facing each other. The remaining workstations are placed 'shoulder by shoulder' facing the large panorama windows.

One can imagine that this office layout would – almost by itself – create a certain amount of interaction between the members. But management has taken the network ambition one step further. It has set the rule that the members must clear their desks completely every night, and that each member must sit in a new place every day. In this way, the argument goes, every member will automatically generate a broad array of contacts.

The rule of changing place has an interesting history, which I have been able to track in broad outline. When United Spaces started about one year ago, the managers insisted strongly on the rule, and they reminded the members to change place when they found them at the same workstation for more than one day. After a while, one manager told me, they became more pragmatic, in part because the members got annoyed, and in part because the managers didn't like the policing role they found themselves in. So the managers began to ignore the members who didn't move around. And the managers began to accept practical reasons, such as the inconvenience of moving large computer screens.

When I came to United Spaces, nine months after the opening, new members were introduced to the rule as if it were the given order of things. However, as a new member, I quickly discovered that a number of workstations were booked. Papers and personal belongings that were left at the tables from one day to the next indicated this. Some of the more experienced members pointed out to me that the office space was stratified in a peculiar way. The rectangular room seemed to be roughly divided into three sections. IT people dominated one end. Younger, sales-oriented people mostly occupied the middle part of the room. And finally, consultants mostly used the third part of the room. When people did move to a different workstation, they tended to move within rather than between sections.

As a final twist to the story, I shall mention the one place where the rule still exists in a clear form. In the numerous portraits of United Spaces in Danish newspapers and magazines, the rule of changing tables seems to be mentioned every single time. These articles are based on interviews with the managers, who explain the business concept of United Spaces. The journalists seem to find that the rule is a convenient way to explain the unique culture of United Spaces. Judging from the articles, no journalist has ever visited United Spaces for more than one day.

The story about the managerial rule indicates a tension between versions of networking. The rule attempts to focus on and increase interaction among members. In accordance with the club version of networking, equality is attempted: everybody should have equal access to the resources of others. Everybody should conduct his or her networking in the same way. Moreover, the managerial strategy is club-like, in the sense that it attempts to generate interaction internally, that is among the club members; the strategy is unconcerned with relations to outsiders.

The managerial strategy collides with the version of networking which I have called networking-as-acquaintances, and which is indicated by the flow of people, papers and signals across the boundaries of the building. This version of networking is not premised on equality, and it does not distinguish between inside and outside. More over, this rhizomatic network does not move or stay according to any predictable or controllable pattern.

So how is this tension lived with in real-time? The story indicates a series of practical arrangements. First, the managers exert pressure, which is quickly turned into mild pressure, because they don't want to enter into a confrontation with the members. Second, there is a separation of where the rule is applied; it is explained to new members, whereas a blind eye is turned when it comes to the old members. Thirdly, a quite ingenious mode of co-existence is worked out. The members go along with the rule, thus performing the kind of unselective openness desired by managers, but at the same time the members stay largely within their 'section' of the office space, that is with the people with whom they are acquainted the most. Finally, a second separation is taking place. Network-as-acquaintance is allowed to dominate the daily practice at United Spaces, whereas the club-like rule about continual movement and mingling is relegated to the realm of stories told to journalists with the aim of 'branding' United Spaces.

Between Chain and Acquaintances

The third and final pair of network versions consists of chain versus acquaintances. Again one can imagine various tensions between the relatively undirected and undisciplined acquaintance network, and the functional and formalized chain version of network. I shall begin with a story where the tension between the two is unmistakable.

> Uninvited café guests
> Maria tells about an acquaintance who is a very insistent networker. On one occasion, Maria had arranged to meet with her acquaintance in a café. The acquaintance showed up, but in addition to this, the acquaintance had invited several other people. One arrived 10 minutes later, another 20 minutes later, and so on. These people, Maria's acquaintance believed, might be interesting for Maria to talk to, or it might be interesting for them to talk to Maria. Maria found this very annoying because she really went to the café to meet with her acquaintance. Maria uses the word 'acquaintance' intentionally. A friend, she says, would never be that pushy.

In this story, a network of acquaintances is deliberately used to arrange situations where parties meet with the aim of using each other in a specific, that is chain-like way. Maria rejects this blending in a way that resembles the earlier story about the lawyer who made an uninvited sales talk. Both of these stories indicate that in a number of instances, the chain version of network is considered highly inappropriate. Don't mix friendship with business, as the saying goes.

However, there are also times and places where the chain network seems to work in isolation without any interference with other versions of network. Consider this example:

> Automatic discounts
> The manager explains that he has negotiated a discount with the largest Danish telecommunication company (TDC). TDC has defined a zone which contains United Spaces and its immediate surroundings. Within this zone, mobile phone calls are only charged the price of hardwire calls. So anyone with a TDC phone, who visits or works at United Spaces, will automatically get a discount.

With this arrangement – which reportedly works smoothly – a functional chain is established. It includes TDC, the manager of United Spaces, members and visitors, their phone bills, and who knows what technical gadgets. All the different entities do different things, they stick to their roles, and the phone services, payments and discounts flow along regularized channels. The point is that the whole network has been formalized into a functional chain. And in this process, the network has for all practical purposes been separated from a fuzzy network of acquaintances. The discount system does not grow and change incessantly like a network of acquaintances. On the contrary, it works consistently and predictably, month after month.

I have now presented two examples of an adverse relationship between the acquaintance version and the chain version of network. First, a café guest who does not appreciate being approached as a potential business partner. Second and by contrast, a discount system that formalizes and automates a chain of exchanges, while completely ignoring relations of acquaintance. Although these two versions of network are at times separated, one may also imagine that they are sometimes related. After all, there is no end to accounts of business that stress the importance of personal relationships. Alluding to the examples above, one might ask: how is business invited into the friends' network? And how is the rhizomatic network of acquaintances used without disturbing the straight lines of commercial exchange? One possible answer to these questions might be suggested in the following story:

Exchanging external money between friends
Peter explains that he always tries to 'pass on quality'; when he receives a good delivery from a supplier, he recommends this supplier to a friend. A series of benefits follows from this:

1. Peter does his friend a favour by linking him to a good supplier.
2. Peter gets additional information on the performance of the supplier from his friend (Is the supplier consistently good?)
3. The supplier might in turn start to recommend Peter as a return favour for the business that Peter has generated for the supplier.

This entire series of events means that Peter and his friends are making exchanges without buying or selling among themselves. Peter explains: 'The point is always to get external money into the network of friends', 'You shouldn't suck on each other' (*sic*).

The personal networking strategy outlined by Peter, relates chains (in the form of buyer and seller relations) and acquaintances (in the form of friends) in several interesting ways. To begin, one might observe that the sequence of events indicates a pattern of alternation. First step: a commercial relation between Peter and a buyer. Second step: a friendly sharing of information. Third step: a commercial relationship between the supplier and Peter's friend.

Fourth step: another friendly sharing of information. The chain and the acquaintance version of network are interwoven step by step. However, it is also interesting to note that the two versions of network remain distinct. Money does not enter the relationship between Peter and his friend at any time; it is simply an exchange of information. In a similar vein, the supplier makes a strictly commercial exchange with both Peter and his friend; there is nothing in Peter's story to suggest that particular favours or discounts are involved. In the set of relations that are worked out, the two versions of network are enabling each other without interfering. One could perhaps talk about a benign form of mutual parasitism (compare Serres 1982); the network of friends is able to take something (information) from the commercial relationship, and the commercial relationship is able to take something (identification of potential buyers) from the friend's network. 'You shouldn't suck on each other', Peter says. Exactly. But sucking information from a commercial relationship works fine. And it also works fine to invite a network of commerce to suck at specific nodes in the friends network. In this way, yet another practical way of living with the tension between two versions of network has been worked out.

DISCUSSION

In the previous sections, three different versions of network (club, chain and acquaintance) have been outlined and practical ways of living with tension between these versions have been explored. In this way, the analysis attempts to give an empirical answer to the theoretical question of how it is possible to reconcile the different versions of network.

A number of answers have been suggested. First of all, it is evident that the different versions are separated in a number of instances: being allergic to sales speeches; shredding documents so that information doesn't flow; frowning at uninvited café guests; making a closed automatic system; telling one story to the new members and the press, while performing a different one with the older members; and in everyday practice. All of these practices or events are ways to separate different versions of network, and thus practical ways of living with difference. Contrary to at least some popular ideas about United Spaces, it is not a boundaryless place. It is a place that produces a number of boundaries: boundaries between business and friends, between old and new members, and between branding and everyday life.

So separation is one way of living with tension. But as we have seen, there is also a number of cases in which different versions of network are combined in ways that make it possible to perform both versions at the same time. Three examples of this have been discussed. First, the process of making ideas and skills visible, which is then responded to with a specific suggestion, which in turn may lead to a chain-like relationship between club members. Second, the movement patterns of the members: they accommodate the managers' wish for 'equal networking' by moving frequently, although mostly inside specific sections of acquaintances. Third, a personal strategy of networking has been outlined; this strategy continuously interweaves friends and business partners without ever fusing the two. In the process, a benign form of mutual parasitism is developed between on the one hand friends and acquaintances and on the other hand business partners and chain-like relationships.

Whether separation or some complicated form of combination is the case, the analysis above is informed by the image of a full world. Networking is not about filling a void. Networking is an emerging pattern of difference, tensions and occasional reconciliation between different versions of network. If this pattern of tensions is the practice through which identity is performed, then it is possible to draw a rather sharp contrast to the view of identity that comes with a notion of networking or 'network society' as a free and open space.

A clear example of this latter view is illustrated in an article by Daniel Pink (1998). Pink writes in the American Internet Magazine *Fast Company*, on the topic of self-employed North Americans, which he believes is a rapidly growing segment of the workforce.[7] He calls this workforce 'free agents' and depicts it as a liberation movement. 'Free agents quickly realised that in a traditional world, they were silently accepting an architecture of work customs and social mores that should have crumbled long ago under the weight of their own absurdity'. However, as a free agent, Pink says, 'work is personal. You can achieve a beautiful synchronicity between who you are and what you do'. Later he quotes one of his informants as saying, 'people [that is free agents] assume their own shape rather than fit the shape of some corporate box'.

In Pink's account, identity is an inner determination or shape, which will come out, in the absence of social constraints. Pink believes that self-employed Americans are indeed realizing their inner selves, which must by implication mean that their working lives take place in some sort of vacuum, or in a world which they can arrange 'personally'.

This account of identity as self-fulfilment in the absence of external constraints is contradicted by the present account of practice at United Spaces. The continuing point of the analysis is that you are always up against something; the absence of tension or the absence of others is an absurdity. This means that identities emerge relationally, that is with or against something. The relational formation of identity is an aspect of on-going practice. And in the case of United Spaces, I argue that this practice can be described as a pattern of separation and combination of different versions of network. In the following, I relate the account of practice at United Spaces to the major conceptualizations of identity which were outlined at the beginning of this chapter (subjectification, belonging, personal history). I shall discuss how practice at United Spaces produces particular forms of identity.

Subjects of Offering and Mutual Visibility

In *Discipline and Punish*, Michel Foucault links the development of character to the construction of various kinds of visibility. The omnipresent threat of surveillance leads to self-monitoring, which turns the self into a prison. Drawing on this panoptical perspective, one could argue that United Spaces constructs a particular kind of visibility. In particular, the network arena and the rule of changing tables are designed to make the members visible and available to each other. However, there is an important difference to note. In the case of the Panopticon, the surveyor is hidden and perhaps absent. But in the case of United Spaces, the surveyor and the surveyed are one and the same. The set-up at United Spaces produces an inter-opticon – the visibility of all to all – rather than a Panopticon. The consequences of an inter-opticon regime must be different. It must require a different set of strategies of self. Several examples have been mentioned: the strategy of making one's ideas and skills visible, the strategy of making specific suggestions to others, and the strategy of avoiding ('being allergic to') interactions that formalize the relationships too quickly. The common theme running through these examples might be about 'offering'. The relationship to others is not a matter of control and submission or a matter of rights and obligations. Inter-subjective relatedness is about making offers, and being offered something. This economy of 'offers' constructs a positive atmosphere of pleasing, and perhaps an atmosphere where negative or aggressive emotions and talk are shunned. This apparently open and sharing environment may then come with, or indeed depend on, a self-discipline aimed at being likeable and pleasant. In this regime, the greatest threat is to be ignored and abandoned: the ever-present possibility that no one will accept your offers and that no one will offer you anything.

Identity between Ambiguous Social Worlds

Notions of communities (Lave and Wenger 1991) or social worlds (Strauss 1978) have often been used to anchor the notion of identity. Solid identity is about belonging. The formation of identity is about socialization and enculturation. This view of identity implies that the world is described as a mosaic of minor orders. If this image is applied to United Spaces, we might quickly point to the three 'sections of acquaintances' as social worlds. However, the cases which have been discussed in this chapter suggest a somewhat more complicated picture. It may well be that acquaintances form particular 'social worlds'. But it also appears that acquaintances tend to be rather unlimited and to grow in all directions, which runs counter to the image of a patch in a mosaic. Even more confusingly, the patch that *is* bounded, the club of United Spaces, seems to be held together with quite some difficulty. The members subdivide themselves and maintain countless links that evade the community which the managers attempt to create. So it appears that the communities at United Spaces have rather loose edges and even more significantly, it seems that every individual is entangled with several. The story about the rule of changing table vividly illustrates that the members simultaneously play the game of being members and of belonging to a network of acquaintances. The idea of identities, solidly planted in a social world, is thus challenged at United Spaces. It seems that individuals emerge in a rather messy borderland between many different communities that are ambiguously defined as well.

Identities and Non-linear Modes of Accumulation

Writing within the branch of identity theorizing that focuses on personal histories, Richard Sennett has recently argued(1998) that character corrodes in the new economy. This corrosion, he argues, is linked to the fact that accumulation is no longer possible. In earlier times, it was possible to get a steady job that made it possible to provide for a family and predict income and savings all the way to retirement. Sennett's claim is that accumulation, and hence a stable character, is no longer possible. Constant changes of jobs, career paths and physical locations destroy the possibility of accumulation.

Apparently, there is much in Sennett's account that resonates with the workings of United Spaces: the constant relocation in the office space, the frequent coming and going of members and the insecurity related to small start-up firms. However, there is at least one case story that suggests that accumulation is possible, even under these conditions. Peter's story on exchanging external money with his friends, does indeed suggest a pattern of accumulation. A commercial relationship is made into something in the friends network, which leads to more business, which then leads to more exchanges in the friends network. Peter is in fact accumulating, but he does this in a very peculiar way. He constantly shifts between the commercial and the friends network, always adding something more. Where Sennett's 'character' accumulates (commercial) income in a linear fashion, Peter's movement is zigzagging. Every exchange he makes is followed by a sharp bend and continues in a different direction. This, one could argue, does not provide the long-term predictability which Sennett takes to be the basis of a good life. But Peter does collect a rather self-perpetuating crowd of links, which constantly generate new opportunities for giving and receiving offers. This does not make Peter's life predictable, but it does lower and spread his risks considerably. In this way, Peter achieves a certain stability of character (or at least ease of mind), not because he can predict his path into the future, but because all of his contacts are unlikely to fail him at the same time.

CONCLUSION

United Spaces, an office hotel in Copenhagen that calls itself a network office, is an organization that strives to be an exemplar case of a network environment. In this organization, networking appears in a number of different versions. Networking-as-a-club is based on similarity and boundedness. Networking-as-a-chain is based on difference and functional relations. Networking-as-acquaintances is rhizomatic and productively undefined. The three versions of networking include, exclude and arrange matters differently, and therefore there are tensions between them. However, there are also a number of ways of living with these differences, which at the end of the day makes United Spaces an established disorder.

The tensions, mutual exclusions and partial connections between different versions of networking construct a particular set of practices, which imply particular forms of identity. First of all, United Spaces is characterized by an economy of offering. Commercial collaborations are established by offering the visibility of ideas and skills, and by offering suggestions to others. This is related to an architecture of visibility that makes everybody visible to everybody else, and generates a self-discipline aimed at being positive, likeable and pleasant. The economy of offering is located in a landscape of multiple interleaved and ambiguously defined social communities. For this reason, subjects cannot 'assume' the shape of one or a few social communities. The giving and receiving of offers is located in a complex space of multiple 'communities', some of which do not even produce boundaries (for example, the chain and the acquaintance versions of network). However, predictability or relative security are not ruled out; it is possible to accumulate in a zigzagging rather than in a linear fashion. Different forms of networking may be related by using one form of exchange to benefit other forms of exchange and *vice versa*. The character and the form of security thus generated are based on the compilation of a large number of loosely related connections, rather than on one secure path into the future.

From the arguments above, it follows that identity in a network environment is neither undetermined nor a quality freely emerging from within. Specific forms of identity are enabled and specific other forms of identity are undermined. A network environment like United Spaces is emphatically not the end of external influence on identity. It is a specific reworking of the conditions of identity, a new way of living with tension.

NOTES

1. There are many examples of authors that claim a big difference between old and new forms of work, for example Richard Sennett's claim about the corrosion of character in the contemporary world, and Daniel Pink's rather opposite claim that 'free agents' in the new economy assume 'their own shape rather than the shape of corporate box'.
2. For example, Pink (1998) and Kelly (1999).
3. Concerns are sometimes raised, that homepages simply carry managerial actions or perspectives. This reservation, however, assumes a strict separation of the perspectives of management and the perspectives of everybody else. But even if one does assume that managers would like to order the world in one particular way that differs from all others, then it is still likely that other modes of ordering will permeate the talk and writing of managers. 'Others' may become visible in the form of alternatives that need to be rhetorically undermined, handled in certain ways, or fitted into particular positions (compare Edwards and Potter 1992). For this reason, company homepages, though undoubtedly biased, are still likely to be an interesting source of information on attempts to order the world of a particular company.
4. The notions of *region*, *network* and *fluid* in Mol and Law (1994) closely resemble the notions of club, chain and acquaintance respectively. There are two reasons for not using Mol and Law's terms directly: (1) Mol and Law reserve a specific theoretical meaning for the term 'network'. However, in the present case study the term network is deeply ingrained in the talk, texts, actions and ideology of United Spaces. The practical proliferation of the network term makes it reasonable to treat it as a broad lay term that must be explored, rather than a narrow theoretical term that can be defined and defended. (2) The *modus operandi* of this chapter is to relate empirical material to a number of ideal types. I have found that this analytical approach is much more workable if the ideal types resonate with the way in which stories are told at United Spaces. Despite these differences of approach, the present chapter is profoundly inspired by Mol and Law's analysis of topology.
5. Public lecture by Zygmunt Bauman, Copenhagen Business School, 29 April 2002.
6. *Idee zu einer allgemeinen Geschichte in weltbürgerlicher Absicht*, 1784.
7. Brown and Duguid (2002, xiv) have pointed out that there is strong evidence to the contrary: According to the US Bureau of Labor Statistics, the number of self-employed Americans actually fell in the period between 1994 and 1999. This period includes the dot.com boom, but misses its collapse.

REFERENCES

Brown, J.S. and P. Duguid (1991), 'Organizational Learning and Communities-of-Practice: Towards a Unified View of Working, Learning, and Innovation', *Organization Science*, **2** (1), 40–57.

Brown, J.S. and P. Duguid (2002), *The Social Life of Information*, 2nd edn, Boston, Mass.: Harvard Business School Press.

Castells, M. (2001), 'The Information Age', afterword in P. Himanen (ed.), *The Hacker Ethic*, New York: Random House.

Deleuze, G. and F. Guattari (1987), *A Thousand Plateaus: Capitalism and Schizophrenia*, Minneapolis: University of Minnesota Press.

Edwards, D. and J. Potter (1992), *Discursive Psychology*, London: Sage.

Foucault, M. (1975/1991), *Discipline and Punish*, Harmondsworth: Penguin Books.

Kelly, K. (1999), *New Rules for the New Economy*, London: Fourth Estate.

Knights, D. and D. McCabe (2000), '"Ain't misbehavin?" Opportunities for Resistance under New Forms of "Quality" Management', *Sociology*, **34** (3), 421–36.

Lave, J. and E. Wenger, (1991), *Situated Learning: Legitimate Peripheral*

Participation, Cambridge: Cambridge University Press.
Law, J. (1994), *Organizing Modernity*, Oxford: Blackwell.
Law, J. (2002), *Aircraft Stories: Decentering the Object in Technoscience*, North Carolina: Duke University Press.
Mol, A. and J. Law (1994), 'Regions, Networks and Fluids: Anaemia and Social Topology', *Social Studies of Science*, **24**, 641–71.
Pink, D.H. (1998), 'The Free Agent Nation', *Fast Company*, December/January (**12**), 131–47.
Rose, N. (1996), 'Identity, Genealogy, History', in S. Hall and P. du Gay (eds), *Questions of Cultural Identity*, London: Sage, pp. 128–50.
Sennett, R. (1998), *The Corrosion of Character*, New York: W.W. Norton & Company.
Serres, M. (1982), *The Parasite*, Baltimore: Johns Hopkins University Press.
Sewell, G. and B. Wilkinson (1992), 'Someone to Watch Over Me: Surveillance, Discipline and the Just-in-time Labour Process', *Sociology*, **26** (2), 271–89.
Star, S.L. (1992), 'The Trojan Door: Organizations, Work, and the "Open Black Box"', *Systems Practice*, **5** (4), 395–410.
Strauss, A. (1978), 'A Social World Perspective', *Studies in Symbolic Interaction*, **1**, 119–28.
Suchman, L. (1987), *Plans and Situated Actions: The Problem of Human–Machine Communications*, Cambridge: Cambridge University Press.
Townley, B. (1996), 'Accounting in Detail: Accounting for Individual Performance', *Critical Perspectives on Accounting*, **7** (5), 565–84.
Wenger, E. (1998), *Communities of Practice: Learning, Meaning, and Identity*, Cambridge: Cambridge University Press.

ACKNOWLEDGEMENTS

I am deeply grateful to the two managers at United Spaces Copenhagen, Tore Wanscher and Rikke Prenter, who welcomed my project and gave me much valuable information. I also wish to thank a number of anonymous members at United Spaces, who shared their insights and stories with me. Finally, I thank a number of friends and colleagues who have commented on earlier versions of this chapter: Sami Boutaiba, Michael Brocklehurst, Paul Duguid, Ulrik Hartmann Gade, Paul du Gay, Astrid Jespersen, David Metz, Signe Svenningsen, Estrid Sørensen, Ann Westenholz and Gill Ursell.

4. Temporary stars – the rise and fall of a talent agency
Lars Strannegård and Ola Bergström

> Founded by a leading HR strategy, search and selection firm and a European venture catalyst company, Execency is set to become the European leader in a new top segment of the booming war for talent market by establishing a supreme free agent network with highly experienced and documented top managers, offering execution power to growth and change projects. Execency – The Executive Agency, will act as an agent for business stars. What in many years has been available only for sport and entertainment stars is now available also for business stars. Execency is an agency for business impact people, who want to combine a challenging and well-rewarded career, with the flexibility and nice lifestyle in a free agent role. (Execency Business Idea, 20 October 2000)

This chapter tells the story of an 'agent for business stars', which we shall call Execency, founded in the year 2000 and dissolved as an individual organization in 2001. According to the founders of Execency, the company was a clear-cut 'new economy case'. They explained that the launch of the company was dictated by economic characteristics that dominated at a particular time. The founders sought to express an identity related to an economic and social order that they found suited their purposes. This is to say that they attempted to legitimize the establishment of the company with a positioning geared toward being a solution to the organizing principles, institutions and technologies that dominated at that particular time. In this chapter we analyse, with the rise and fall of Execency as an empirical illustration, how the discursive construction of an 'epoch' unfolded in practice in a specific company, how an organizational identity containing epochal elements was expressed, and how these epochal discourses contributed to the construction of Execency as a boundary actor.

THE NEW ECONOMY AS AN EPOCH

In the 1990s, the public space began to be filled with actors preaching the message of a new economic order. One of the forerunners, Kevin Kelly, former executive director of *Wired Magazine* and author of the book *Ten*

Rules for the New Economy, stated boldly that what he called 'the new economy' would change our lives dramatically by unleashing opportunities never seen before. Much of the talk about the new emerging world attributed the abrupt changes to the wonders of information technology, and more specifically, the Internet. Ever since the introduction of the concept 'new economy', responses have been characterized by both belief and scepticism. For the 'believers' the development of new technologies, new organizational forms and new dominating actors and institutions would lead to a completely new future. The 'sceptics', on the other hand, more often came to describe the new economy as a 'hype' or a 'bubble'. Eventually, some of the words of warning came true. While we experienced a great expansion of new firms and investments in the IT sector in the second half of the 1990s, the year 2000 marked the beginning of a new turn in the discourse of the new economy. Renowned dot-com companies were all of a sudden in bankruptcy. IT consultants were fired. Free services on the web became problematic, as advertisement revenues were insufficient. As a consequence, many venture capitalists, or 'business angels', who hitherto had been risk taking, withdrew from the dot-coms in search of more profitable investments.

Could, the new economy be seen then as an epoch? Webster's *New World Dictionary* defines an epoch as 1) the beginning of a new and important period in the history of anything, and 2) a period of time considered in terms of noteworthy and characteristic events, developments, persons, and so on. Thereby, an epoch is an age in history associated with certain characteristics. To historians, epochs imply a defined period in time that is characterized by dominating organizing principles, institutions, and technologies. But epochs are discursively constructed – they emerge in discursive practices, collectively, and in retrospect. This suggests that an epoch is a way for people to make sense of the world. To describe a period an epoch implies that it is a period in time with clear characteristics.

According to Alexanderson and Trossmark (1997), to talk of epochs is a way to invoke change. Epochs are constructed through periodization, where episodes are linked in narratives to create meaning. They emphasize the role of actor networks in the construction of epochs. Actor networks may construct an event as the beginning of an epoch; the past is given meaning by developing a story consisting of a series of related episodes. New ideas are given meaning and related to existing practice. This may, according to Alexanderson and Trossmark, be regarded as a way to question the continuity of the existing tradition. If the continuity can be maintained, if the renewal is assimilated into what exists already or fails to come off, the existing epoch is prolonged. On the other hand, if there is discontinuity, the tradition is abandoned, an epoch is established in the past and a new epoch begins. The construction of an epoch constitutes a clarification of which past currently relates to the present. The construction of discontinuity is, according to Alexanderson and Trossmark, a way to incorporate the irrelevant past, which may be put away as a closed epoch. The construction of continuity is, on the other hand, about the open epoch–constructions where the past is given a place as traditions.

During the late 1990s, epochal narratives flourished. Technology-related stocks soared, the business media pumped out portraits of 'new economy companies' and business leaders, and the notion of organization was presented as superseded by the notion of network. The rhetoric of a rupture with the past, of a new epoch, could be found in business leaders' presentations, popular management texts, mass media and scholarly texts. The development of society is described in terms of a movement from post-industrial to postmodern (Kumar 1995), which implies new forms of organizing (Clegg 1990; Bergqvist 1993; Law 1994) and new ways of living and forming identity (Giddens 1991). In the beginning of his already classic volume *The Rise of the Network Society*, Manuel Castells summarized the ongoing social changes:

> A technological revolution, centered around information technologies, is reshaping, at accelerated pace, the material basis of society ... Capitalism itself has undergone a process of profound restructuring, characterised by greater flexibility in management; decentralization and networking of other firms both internally and in their relationship to other firms ... (Castells 1996, p. 1)

To Castells, there is apparently a rapid and profound societal change underway. He presents the current social order as fundamentally new, with epochal features. Epochalist claims do not stand uncontested, however. Some consider the 'new economy' to represent something new and promising, while others consider it only to be business as usual dressed up in a new terminology. We are, however, less concerned with whether a 'new' economy has arrived or not, whether careers are becoming more flexible or not, and whether organizing is becoming more network oriented or hierarchical. Instead we are interested in how these epochalist discourses are used as identity claims. Thus, we do not assume that the new economy *is* an epoch, that is whether claims of fundamental changes in society can be traced in the reality that the speakers talk about. Rather, we want to turn back the epochalist claims on those who express them and draw attention to how they contribute to the construction of identity. Thus, we suggest that the novelty of the new economy is not so much related to the reality that it tries to describe, as to the ways in which it allows actors to express identity. In our analysis of the rise and fall of Execency we will indicate how epochal claims were used in identity construction.

CONSTRUCTION OF IDENTITIES

In one strand of organization theory, identity has been conceptualized as a well-defined set of characteristics that members of an organization believe to be distinguishing to that organization (Albert and Whetten 1985; Alvesson and Björkman 1992). Commonly, individual-focused identity theory is transferred to the organizational level and used metaphorically. Phenomena and relationships in organizations are described using the identity concept, which means that organization theorists do not believe that organizations have an identity, but that organizations are better understood when seen as having identities. This description has its roots in the modernistic conviction that identities can be true and uniform. Organizations have, in essence, a 'core'. The modern concept of identity assumes the existence of a true 'self', which is consistent, tightly held together and genuine. Modern identity includes a correlation between experiences and how those experiences are expressed, a continuity in the lives of the individual and the organization, as well as an engagement in the way in which self is expressed (Brown 1989; Czarniawska 2000a). Alvesson and Björkman (1992) connected individual and organizational identity by identifying four factors that influence the tendencies of an individual to identify itself with an organization. The first looks at how distinct a group's values are. The more distinct, the clearer the identity. The second involves the status of the group. The higher the status, the greater the force of attraction. The third factor is indicated by the object of reference, that is to say, other groups. The stronger the awareness of 'others', the greater the awareness of 'us'. The fourth factor involves the existence of social conditions that allow for group formation. The greater the understanding of similarity, common history and background, the clearer the identity (Ashforth and Mael, 1989).

The modernist conception of a true, genuine, and coherent 'self' has been heavily questioned, however. Several scholars have argued that identities are never entirely stable (Gergen 1989; Shotter 1989, 1993). There are no core identities, nor are there essentialist end goals that individuals or organizations reach after periods of uncertainty. Instead, as several scholars have argued, identities are temporary positions in a constantly ongoing conversation (for example Gergen 1989; Shotter 1989; Davies and Harré 1991; Slugoski and Ginsburg 1990). Arguments, claims, definitions and descriptions that are put forward by actors are performative in the sense that they enable action and make certain claims make sense. Identities are confirmed and rejected in conversation with others. Identities are constructed in a context of critique and motivation, and individuals and organizations engage in interactions with others where these identities are expressed and contested. Identities change constantly depending upon context and who is involved in the narration.

According to Weick (1985), identities are constructed upon the interaction and interplay of people. Identity construction is different depending upon who one talks to, and thus, to change an interactive situation is to change one's identity. This is expressed within an ever-changing, kaleidoscopic environment, and identities are therefore location and time-specific. According to such reasoning, there is a world of ongoing presence; a world without origin or destination, past or future, where it is impossible to find a centre; a world in which all that presents itself is temporary, shifting and local regarding forms of knowledge and experience (Kumar 1995). These conditions of postmodernity are said to have important consequences on how identities are constructed.

In contrast, Czarniawska (2000a) claims that neither the modern nor postmodern identities are the case at present. Instead, action and self-presentation in contemporary organizations are more comparable to pre-modern identity norms. In ancient Rome, identity included taking on a position in society and explicitly being responsible for one's actions (MacIntyre 1981). Following tradition and being respectful of history were Roman virtues, and both were important elements in the construction of identity. This is to say that continuity and coherence were virtues, but not in the modernist sense of the term. Modern identity ideals expect people to be themselves independent of context, while the post-modern concept of identity rejects such notions altogether. The pre-modern ideal claimed that identity did not rest upon the characteristics of personality, but upon one's relationship to the group of people one lived and worked with. Thus, identity construction in the pre-modern era brings in the notion of self-presentation and narration. The position in relation to others, the process of self-presentation and the interpretation by different audiences were in focus. This is similar to how Czarniawska (2000b) views identity construction in contemporary organizational life. Successful identity presentations do not require that today's actions are consistent with yesterday's, but they need some kind of consistency. For instance, a change in identity claims cannot be accepted without explanation; it requires a convincing explanation as to why certain actions have been taken. Hence, contemporary organizational identity might imply a modification of the authenticity requirements of modern identity and the array of multiple identities postulated by the post-modern thought tradition. Identity might be seen as a combination of stability and multiplicity, connected through a convincing narrative.

THE RISE AND FALL OF EXECENCY

In the mid-1990s, when John Johansson was 24 years old and had just finished his master's degree in management, he took a job as a trainee in a Swedish communications company. Within one year he became the CEO of a customer support company and his mission was to increase the revenues by several hundred per cent and take the company to the stock exchange. After three years he had contributed to expanding the service business from 400 to 2000 employees and considered it time to move on. In the spring of 1999, he quit his job and went to Harvard University to study an executive general management program. The summer before, he had attended a program for growing companies at Stanford University and was thrilled by the Silicon Valley region. After finishing his Harvard program, he therefore found it appropriate to go back to Silicon Valley to do interviews and to figure out what was 'hot' in the world's IT Mecca. He noticed the demand for qualified staff in the dot-com companies and the tendency for potential employees to shop around for employment in order to find the best deal as regards exciting projects and financial opportunities. He thought this concept would translate to the emerging dot.com industry in the Swedish mobile valley in the Stockholm region. When he came back to Sweden, he was full of ideas and inspiration, and started to sketch out a few business plans.

Meanwhile, a number of Stockholm consultants from the Boston Consulting Group (BCG) and McKinsey and Company had quit their jobs to form an entrepreneurial venture capital and human resource firm, TREK. The former consultants had earlier worked with different IT, e-venture and high-tech projects, and now decided to start a company that assisted with the formation and support of new business ventures. The consultants recognised talent, specific knowledge and the right networks to be the dominating elements in the creation of a new business. Their experience as consultants also gave them support for the idea that clients, in addition to strategic analysis, needed help in the implementation of the recommendations made by the consultants.

In one of the large Swedish search, selection and HR strategy firms, Campus, the recruitment consultants in the late 1990s experienced what they regarded as a shift in the mind-sets of their highly qualified candidates. The boom in the stock market and drastic increase in newly formed dot-com companies had made high level candidates increasingly demanding. They now wanted ownership in the companies they were to work in, had high salary requirements and were more interested in interesting projects than permanent employment. On the high-end customer side, there were frequent signals of a willingness to pay substantially for human resources that could deliver results quickly. Based on these experiences, some of the recruitment consultants nurtured the thought of some kind of strategic response.

In his former position, Mr Johansson had had contact with some of the BCG and McKinsey consultants, and the recruitment firm knew him from their database of 'top talents'. The former management consultants started to discuss a business idea based on high-achieving individuals, contacted the HR strategy firm Campus, and held a series of meetings, and just a few months after John had returned to Sweden, he was appointed CEO of the newly started company. The company was to be a talent agency for management executives, and it was launched in August 2000 under the name Execency. Execency was to provide its clients with what it called super talents, that is individuals with a track record of excellent achievements in their fields of expertise. The idea was that this group of individuals did not want a permanent employment contract. They regarded themselves as free agents. They did this in order to free themselves from their clients' mismanagement and in order to be able to specialize in their professional fields and plan their own working time. Importantly, the 'stars' were not to be employed by the agency, but to operate their own companies. The agency was to provide 'stars' with assignments, support functions and star-boosting fringe benefits such as platinum credit cards, membership awards and other life-facilitating services.

At the outset, Execency had seven individuals on the payroll. The project-based hire of executives, according to the CEO, enabled organizations to be flexible in their use of talents, and enabled additional top resources in periods of growth or change, in pre-defined projects, in times when there was an extraordinary need for competence or in periods where a temporary gap needed to be filled. Execency would support these individuals in finding new and interesting missions, negotiating fees and carrying out different types of administrative work. But in order to put this business idea into practice, financial support from investors was needed.

In the following section we will analyse the characteristics of the Execency identity claims and their relation to the epochal discourse. The following presentation is based on interviews with talents and agency managers between November 2000 and March 2001, on studies of sales-pitch presentations to potential stars and clients, on all mass media material where Execency was featured, and on internal documentation.

The business idea of Execency was based on two general discourses: a discourse on how labour markets change and a discourse on how industries change in the new economy. Both discourses had epochalist features, describing the conditions of the future in relation to the past.

Talk about Labour Market Change

The business idea of Execency was based on a number of discursive elements with epochalist features. The founders described Execency in terms of a number of 'driving forces' that would put the firm in a position to be a solution to problems in the labour market. First, the labour force was said to have become increasingly flexible and mobile.

> Execency – The Talent Agency, will act as an agent for business stars. What in many years has been available only for sport and entertainment stars, is now available also for business stars. Execency is an agency for business impact people, who want to combine a challenging and well-rewarded career, with the flexibility and nice lifestyle in a free agent role. [Execency presentation material November 2000]

This was supported by different 'historical facts' concerning changes in the labour market. For example, the CEO stated that the average time an employee held a position had decreased from 23 years during the 1950s to four years during the late 1990s. These 'facts' were interpreted as evidence of an increased focus on life quality and self-fulfilment among workers. This development was explained by arguing that individuals change jobs because they want to develop personally and learn something new. The founders also thought that there was an emerging change in the attitude towards employment security among workers:

> The downsizing of the 1980s and 1990s has changed the attitudes toward job security. A permanent job or position is no guarantee for job security, but a unique competence is. Top talents are hard to find and expensive to employ to a permanent position. These top-achieving individuals often want to be independent and are interested in self-fulfilment and a flexible life style. They have no interest in life-long employment since they know that they perform well. Therefore, they are interested in receiving a large proportion of their compensation based on the result they deliver. Execency will enable individuals to develop an individual career path where they could capitalize fully on their competence and enable them to build their own brands. (Marketing manager, December 2, 2000)

This sense of changing attitudes and emerging disloyalty to employers was regarded as a support for the business idea of Execency. For the founders it seemed self-evident that both employers and employees would be interested in engaging an agency like Execency to satisfy their needs in the new economy. Execency could provide talents with the security they needed while capitalizing on their competence.

The founders also referred to articles describing the labour market as a 'war for talents'. In particular, one of the founders mentioned the article 'The War for Talent' in *The McKinsey Quarterly*. According to this article, attraction, recruitment, and development of key competencies had become strategic success factors for firms in the new economy.

> The most important corporate resource over the next 20 years will be talent. It's also the resource in shortest supply – Ed Michels, McKinsey and Co (from Execency presentation material December 2000)

Drawing on metaphors of war, the article stated that the 'war for talent' would be intensified during the coming years. In order to support this claim in the Swedish context, reference to labour force statistics on changes in the composition of the work force were made. Within 15 years, the CEO argued, the number of Europeans aged between 35 and 45 would decrease by 15 per cent. During this period the economy would be likely to grow by 3 to 4 per cent per year. Since the 35 to 45 age group is the primary executive management target group, the demand for executive talent would increase by 25 per cent while the supply of appropriate talent would decrease with 15 per cent. As a consequence, talent management should be regarded as a top priority. References were also made to predictions that executives would become more interested in flexibility regarding lifestyle choices, and that talents would demand more performance-related compensation. In order to support this, Execency representatives referred to 'new ideas' among American economists regarding the development of individualized stock markets:

> One of the major new financial instruments will involve the securitization of individuals. In the early Industrial Age, we created securities for large corporations. Then, early in the Information Age, we developed a stock market for fast-growth, startup companies. Now there are 'microcaps' – smaller and smaller entities for capitalization. The ultimate logic leads to a market for the individual, a stock in a person. Stan Davis [Quotation from Execency sales pitch]

These predictions and statements concerning the future labour market were taken as a basis for the need for Execency. If these predictions were true, employers would soon realize their needs and be willing to buy services that would help them to fight the war for talent.

In sum, as these documents and statements show, representatives of the company defined Execency through what they regarded as changes in the labour market. In particular, changes were described in terms of an epochal shift. There were clear distinctions between the conditions of the future (talents as a strategic success factor, new values and preferences among talents) and the past (a focus on job security and long-term employment relationships).

Talk about Industrial Change

The definition of Execency also included talk about industrial change. Presentations to investors and clients included detailed predictions and descriptions of how the new economy would change the conditions for firms. The new economy was described as having considerable impact on the way business was constructed.

> The talent market is undergoing substantial change driven by increased focus by

companies on value creation, the need to rapidly build or re-build businesses. [Execency slide show to talent prospects, January 2000]

Continuous change in the new economy required firms to organize work more and more in terms of projects. According to the CEO, there was a trend toward project-based work and a need for project management skills.

> Overall, top management performance is now more transparently impacting results and work is increasingly performed as projects. In addition, companies/projects have more differentiated needs for execution support over time while project time phases get only shorter. (CEO, February 2001)

This meant that the project, not the position in the hierarchy – as in the 'old economy' – needed to be staffed. In his view, many companies needed a competent person in a growth phase or in a change project, but when the project was over, the talent was still a cost since he or she had been recruited to a position, not a project. This 'trend' was taken as evidence that the volume of talent needed to be flexible. Yet, said the CEO, this did not imply that traditional positions were obsolete. Instead, Execency was described as 'a complement to the ordinary staff'. Each organization needs to have permanent employees and hire extra talents from time to time to boost the company development.

References were made to descriptions of the American film industry as an example of an industry that had already adopted the structure and principles of the network economy.

> Hollywood [has mutated] from an industry of classical huge vertically integrated corporations into the world's best example of a network economy ... Eventually, every knowledge-intensive industry will end up in the same flattened atomized state. Hollywood just has gotten there first. Joel Kotkin, Inc. Magazine [quotation from Execency sales pitch]

The fierce war for talent was, according to the Execency founders, a US phenomenon, and was about to boom on the European labour market.

> Head start for Execency in 'Wireless Valley' and internationalisation across Europe. Execency is being started with a first hub in Stockholm with its booming need for project based top execution power. (Execency presentation to investors, November 2000)

The war for talent was also, according to the marketing manager, driven by the increased entrepreneurial activity of the new economy. The newly started IT ventures in the Stockholm area had demanded executives that were able to make companies grow rapidly. Sweden was regarded as a test case for the

Execency business idea. But soon the concept was to be expanded to other European countries.

> Campus's *Professional Network* provides an excellent head start with a lead case and significant PR coverage. Execency is set to establish and rollout its business model in 8 European countries, with assistance from leading venture capitalists, Trek and Campus. (Execency presentation to investors, November 2000)

In sum, Execency was defined by identifying epochal changes in the structure and functioning of business. The future was described as occupied by start-up firms and knowledge-based industries, organized in project-based activities, while the past consisted of large rigid corporations with little potential for adaptation and survival.

Going to Battle

Execency was not only characterized by epochal discourses; there were also descriptions of a number of practices or activities that would facilitate the process of mediating the interests of talents and the clients' demand for talents. In order to participate in 'the war for talents', Execency needed to attract talented people that they could transfer to clients.

> Execency's target is to have 500 active top management free agents within two years and 2000–3000 free agents within 4 years. (Execency presentation to investors, November 2000)

These targets were presented as 'aggressive but realistic'. They also needed to make sure that talents had the promised qualifications. In order to achieve this, an extensive classification system was developed. The list of qualifications was divided into four parameters: educational background, professional experience, competence and personality. The requirement for the educational background was an 'Ivy League' (in this context meaning a top school in the country) academic degree. The professional background needed to be between five and twenty years in consulting, management, IT or start-up experience. Most importantly, in order to qualify as a talent, a track record of documented executive power was needed. It was necessary to have extensive experience of growth and change projects. Following on from the professional experience, the competence needed to be in the fields of general management, entrepreneurship or specialist competence such as having held a position as Chief Financial Officer or Chief Technological Officer. The final parameter, personality, required talents to be flexible, confident, entrepreneurial, non-prestigious, non-political and hands-on. Each individual was classified according to the possible role that he or she could perform for clients:

innovators, settlers, dealmakers, permanent team members, turnaround artists and second generation builders. Thus, talents were classified according to a common scheme and packaged in a way that would enable them to be matched to clients dependent on the client's position in the business life cycle.

Right from the beginning, the representatives of Execency started to search for 'talents' to sign on as members of their network. First of all, individuals in the databases of the search firm were screened. Later they broadened their scope to include suitable candidates who either approached Execency or existed in the broad network of the representatives of the company. In order to find individuals that fulfilled the Execency criteria, an extensive screening process was put in place, including pre-studies, first selections, interviews, psychological assessments, reference checks and tests. By October 2000, six hundred individuals had been screened, and thirty offered a place in the network. By the same date, two talents had been out on assignment.

Despite the high qualification requirements, there were no problems finding talents to sign up as members. The offer was very beneficial for the candidates and there were no risks associated with being a member of the network. According to one of the talents, having Execency as an agent enabled different projects to be undertaken in different companies for shorter periods of time. Working through Execency was regarded as making life more challenging, but at the same time with conditions adjusted to the individual. Execency made it easier to get balance in life since it made it possible to take long breaks between missions, and took the boring administrative work away, including negotiating fees. 'Thereby', said the talent, 'it becomes easier to focus on what I am good at, and let somebody else handle things like negotiating fees and keeping books.' Thus, Execency's promise of offering talents a way to deal with the conditions of the new economy was regarded as highly attractive.

All stars in the Execency network had their own companies, and the agent service included company formation administration, book keeping, secretary service and travel arrangements. Execency handled all negotiations with clients and took care of contracts and paperwork. In addition, a number of, as the CEO put it, 'prima-donna' fringe benefits had been added. These included platinum American Express cards and VIP cards to a number of bars and clubs in Stockholm. Thus, there were no problems for Execency to attract talents. This gave them courage to go into battle in the 'war for talents'.

Second, in order to facilitate the transfer of the right person to the right job, there was also extensive information gathering and analysis of the client's workplace. Together with the client, the agency was to formulate a project and profile analysis. The purpose of this was to find out where in the business life cycle the client was positioned and the kind of competencies needed to do the job. This would facilitate the transfer of a person with the right profile and ensure both satisfied clients and talents. Clients were analysed according to a classification scheme in which they could be placed in six different phases. These were innovation, animation, acceleration, maturity, change and the second acceleration phase. The phases required different types of talent. The corresponding talents needed in the phases were innovators, settlers, deal makers, permanent team members, turnaround artists and second generation builders. Execency focused on four of the phases: animation, acceleration, change and the second acceleration phase. These phases were regarded as most relevant in the context of the new economy. They include both new enterprises – start-ups – that would need competence in order to grow in the new economy and old-economy organizations that would need competence in order to change and turn around their businesses.

In the animation phase, the agency was to provide settlers, who could typically work to recruit others, raise seed money, and build and sell the first products. In the next phase, deal makers could work to raise capital, build the brand, work with marketing and sales, expand internationally and continuously focus on business development. Companies that had matured usually experienced a dip in turnover and profitability and needed some kind of reorientation. In such instances Execency could provide turnaround artists who reorganized, reduced costs, initiated mergers and acquisitions, and renegotiated prices. After such a turnaround, second generation builders were appropriate. These were to redefine the strategy, reposition the company and/or the products, and start rebuilding the marketing and sales functions.

A typical assignment was to be IT manager, marketing manager, chief financial officer, sales manager or qualified project manager. The agency formulated a specification of the assignment and an offer. The agency was to take 10 per cent in commission from both the talent and the client. If the offer was accepted, the agency matched the profile against the talents. Within a week the client received a notice and a description of the matched talent. If the talent was interested, the agency set up a meeting between the talent, the client and the agency. Until this stage, the process had been of no cost to the client. If all parties were interested in proceeding, the agency administered, negotiated and set up the necessary contracts. The cost for this phase was $2500 US. After this, the project started, and the talent was on her or his own. During the project, the agency would assess and give feedback continuously on the development, and when the project was terminated, which would typically be between six and eighteen months later, the agency would undertake a final assessment of both sides.

The Lost Battle

By November 2002, Execency no longer existed as a company of its own. TREK and John Johansson sold their parts to Campus, which turned Execency

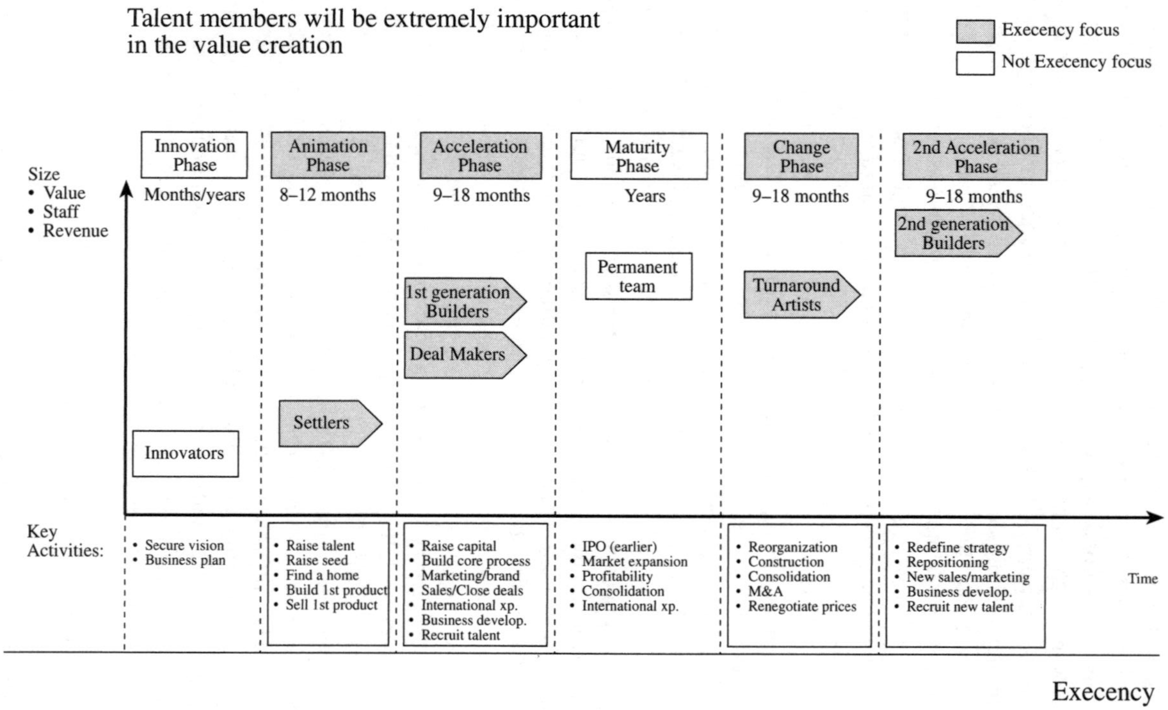

Figure 4.1 Execency's presentation to investors, talents and customers

into an Campus product among others. According to the founders, the driving forces behind this development (just like the forces behind the formation) were manifold. The main reason was, according to the founders, that the market prerequisites were lacking. The founders spoke of the Execency idea as a financial one. The initial idea was to make Execency quickly pan-European:

> Execency was a 'new economy' case. We wanted to grow as quickly as possible in order to spread our brand everywhere. Initially we were a company completely geared toward the venture capitalists. The Venture Capitalists needed talents to put in the companies they had invested in. [Marketing director, 1 November 2002]

When Execency went to venture capitalists for money, as one of the founders said, timing was bad. The stock market had been going down for a number of months, and when investors were finally attracted, they first lowered the price substantially. And even though a letter of intent was signed, Ericsson, by then the most important actor in the Swedish economy as a whole, declared that all consultant contracts were to be terminated. At this time, the venture capitalists withdrew, and left Execency without options. The first strategy had thus been to approach venture capitalists and aim at rapid growth. When this option turned out to be unsuccessful, the next strategy was to approach the potential clients, that is large Swedish companies:

> We were shocked. The large companies all said no. They say no to all managers that are not permanently employed. Even though we had a network of 70–80 highly qualified talents, it was impossible for us to get in. [CEO, 1 November 2002]

During 2001, Execency found talents to be a scarce resource. The new economic situation had instead turned assignments and the promised need for talents into scarcity. When Execency was founded, its business idea was to be a resource for the talents, and Hollywood and sport stars were used as metaphors. Suddenly, although the network of talents was growing smoothly, the assignments did not come in. And that made the talents lose trust, as one of the former members of Execency expressed it:

> I am used to finding my own projects, and Execency was supposed to give me support. But at that time (Spring 2001) the projects proposals were scarce, and Execency did not help me. Why would I need them in that case? (Former member of Execency network. [Quoted by CEO, 1 November 2002])

In 2001, the CEO began to question whether Execency would be able to deliver what was promised. There were ongoing projects; the turnover in 2001 was some 800 thousand US dollars from eight projects (implying 160 thousand US dollars for Execency), and break-even was reached. Yet it became clear that venture capitalists were not willing to spend money, and the projects were hard to find. Furthermore, when assignments were scarce, talents might well take the opportunity to accept offers of permanent employment in order to secure employment rather than going through the talent agency. Thus, when talents and clients could meet without the mediation of the agency, the strong distinction between demand and supply and past and future, which was the basis for the identity of Execency, could not be reproduced. By the end of 2001, it became clear that the situation was unsustainable. Campus acquired the shares from TREK and John Johansson, and achieved 100 per cent ownership of Execency. At present, Execency is described on the Campus web site as under 'interim management'. It is still a network of individuals, but the Execency network is seen as somewhat of a side activity and not the core business for Campus.

EXECENCY AS A BOUNDARY ACTOR

The rise and fall of Execency can be understood through Execency's identity claims. When added together, Execency was first and foremost a series of utterances, a number of claims about future developments and about the past. These claims were similar in the sense that they were all constructed around an epochal change. It was argued that in order to be a part of the new economy, firms need to turn around their organizational structure and take part in the war for talents. For the 'new economy organizations', start-ups and knowledge-intensive organizations, there was a need to get access to highly skilled professionals. Similar stories were told to investors, clients and talents: the new economy implies that highly skilled workers will be in high demand and that there is a trend among highly talented people to be independent and develop their personal brand. Epochalist claims were characterized by descriptions of what the reality would be like in the future, statements about the past and definitions of what would be needed in the future. There were also descriptions of the nature of the intermediary business and the services provided. References were made to the expansion of a number of internet-based marketplaces mediating consultant services in the United States and Europe (Monster, Guru.com, FreeAgent.com, Elance, Hellobrain, Ants, Aquent, and so on), as if Execency was an example of a growing industry that would flourish in the future. These kinds of descriptions were used to attract financial support for the business and also to attract clients and talents. This is to say that Execency consisted of not much more than well-motivated definitions of what the organization 'was' and what it was supposed to do (Salzer 1994). Hence, the representatives of Execency delivered identity claims based on the arrival of a new epoch.

This epochal shift was described in terms of both changes in the labour market and the structure and functioning of business. These discourses are put together in a common story presented in relation to clients and talents. However, despite the common features, the epochalist discourses identify tensions between the different social worlds: the world of business and the world of talents. Or, as the CEO put it:

> There are so many market imperfections in the labour market. It's hard for companies to know where to find the talents. And if a company finds them, the star usually does not get the compensation he or she is worth. Also, growth phases and change projects need to be staffed directly. But usually, talents cannot leave their permanent positions quicker than after six months. And then it is usually too late.

Execency offered an opportunity to resolve these tensions by analysis, categorization and classification of both clients and talents. Execency was defined as a mediator that would facilitate the connection between these two worlds. Thus, Execency may be regarded as similar to what Bowker and Star (1999) call a boundary object, that is

> those objects that both inhabit several communities of practice and satisfy the informational requirements of each of them. In working practice, they are objects that are able both to travel across borders and maintain some sort of constant identity. They can be tailored to meet the needs of any one community (they are plastic in this sense, or customizable). At the same time, they have common identities across settings.' (p. 16)

But it may be more useful to speak of Execency as a boundary actor, rather than an object. As a boundary actor, Execency manifested features of several communities (consultancy, recruitment agencies, venture capitalists, client industries, experts, project managers and executives). The practices of Execency – classification schemes, recruitment procedures, profile analysis and book-keeping systems – satisfied the informational requirements of all parties involved, even though they had different meanings depending on the perspective from which they were regarded. By undertaking these activities, Execency could transgress the borders of communities, while maintaining a stable identity. Thus, Execency maintained an identity by defining itself as a boundary actor that transgressed borders both in time and space, between past and present, and between different communities.

There were limitations to the extent to which Execency could maintain the identity as a boundary actor, however. It presupposes that all actors recognized and accepted Execency as a part of their community or social world. According to Czarniawska (2000b), the similarity dimension is the most important aspect of identity construction – that which involves the unique is secondary. The most important thing is to show whom, or what, you resemble.

But in the case of Execency, the reference to what they resembled had the opposite effect. Even if Execency manifested features that would be recognized as 'natural' or familiar to the business communities, there were also features in the description of Execency that could have been regarded as awkward or strange. For example, in sales presentations, metaphors of agents in Hollywood and the sports world were widely used: 'Hollywood has done it for decades, IMG has done it for years. And to Execency, all business is like show business'. In describing its role it referred to other intermediary markets, such as artists, movie stars or sportsmen, where talents are provided with personal service and high salaries. By analogy, the founders described themselves as the business world's equivalent of Hollywood agents. Representatives of Execency kept repeating that the organization was not like other companies, that Execency was something different. The claim that Execency did not belong in 'the old economy' was repeated continuously. Such features may have helped to limit the acceptance of Execency as a part of the business community. Execency was in the position of being similar to something that was not regarded as valuable or accepted. Thus, references to resemblance to other actors rather limited the possibilities for taking on a role as a boundary actor.

Furthermore, the reproduction of identity as a boundary actor presumed that actors or communities were not linked in other ways. For example, there was always a possibility that clients would find the talents they needed or that talents would accept offers of permanent jobs at clients independent of Execency, despite their interest in autonomy and flexibility. Thus, the identity of Execency as a boundary actor required the social worlds of clients and talents to be held separate in time and space.

This also illustrates the conditions and limitations of identity construction based on epochalist discourses. These provided a possibility for making distinctions between actors (those who belong to or take part in the epochal shift and those who do not). Furthermore, the epochalist discourse contains claims about the consequences of not taking part in the epochal shift. Central actors such as start-ups and venture capitalists (actors that were considered to be the backbone for the establishment of a new economy) would need the services of Execency to find workers for their start-ups. Meanwhile, actors of the old economy would need the turnaround artists provided by Execency in order to adjust to the conditions of the new economy that was dawning. If they did not take part in this movement, they would not survive. However, the epochal character of Execency's identity claims implied that Execency was dependent on the realization and manifestation of an epochal shift. If no epochal shift were to appear, Execency would lack legitimacy. This means that the identity of Execency was vulnerable. The organization needed to be able to ensure manifestations of an epochal shift in order to legitimize further investment in the company by venture capitalists and to convince clients to buy their services. In so far as clients, talents and venture capitalists believed in the definition of the broader context, Execency would have been able to turn their ideas into action and profit.

Apparently, the identity claims were more than just an analytic perspective. They appeared to have considerable consequences for the representatives of Execency. The dependence on the arrival of 'the new economy' implied that Execency was completely dependent on something that they could not possibly affect themselves. When the stock market turned down, and when the rhetoric of a new economic order disappeared from the public space, the efforts to convince clients and venture capitalists of the validity of the concept of a new epoch were not sufficient. When the identity claims lose their credibility, the legitimacy base may vanish. Thus, identity constructions based on epochalist discourses are based on claims about reality that are vulnerable to the acceptance and sense making of the other. This means that identity construction is not so much related to a true description of who we are, but rather, as this case illustrates, meaningful descriptions of a world in which we may have a relevant place.

The case of Execency may thus provide us with some general understanding of identity construction in contemporary organizations. Boundary actors neither claim a unique and stable identity, nor a multitude of identities decoupled from each other. Instead, they establish their identity claims by drawing on features of the different contexts that it transgresses. Through examples, comparative narratives and claims of belonging to different organizational fields, the boundary-transgressing identity emerges: stable, yet vulnerable and uncertain.

REFERENCES

Albert, S. and D. Whetten (1985), 'Organizational Identity', in L. Cummings and B. Staw (eds), *Research in Organizational Behavior*, **7**, pp. 263–95.

Alexanderson, O. and P. Trossmark (1997), *Om Konstruktion av Förnyelse*, Lund: Lunds Universitet.

Alvesson, M. and I. Björkman (1992), *Organisationsidentitet och Organisationsbyggande: En Studie av ett Industriföretag*, Lund: Studentlitteratur.

Ashforth, B.E. and F. Mael (1989), 'Social Identity Theory and the Organization', *Academy of Management Review*, **14** (1), pp. 20–39.

Bergqvist, W. (1993), *The Postmodern Organization: Mastering the Art of Irreversible Change*, New York: Jossey Bass Ltd.

Bowker, G.C. and S.L. Star (1999), *Sorting Things Out: Classification and its Consequences*, London: MIT Press.

Brown, R.H. (1989), *Social Science as a Civic Discourse*, Chicago: University of Chicago Press.

Castells, M. (1996), *The Rise of the Network Society* (The Information Age: Economy, Society and Culture, 1), Oxford: Blackwell.

Clegg, S. (1990), *Modern Organizations: Organization Studies in the Postmodern World*, London: Sage.

Czarniawska, B. (2000a), 'The European Capital of the 2000s: On Image Construction and Modeling', *Corporate Reputation Review*, **3** (3), pp. 202–17.

Czarniawska, B. (2000b), 'Identity Lost or Identity Found: Celebration and Lamentation over the Postmodern View of Identity in Social Science and Fiction', in M. Schultz, M.J. Hatch and M.H. Larsen (eds), *The Expressive Organization: Linking Identity, Reputation and the Corporate Brand*, Oxford: Oxford University Press, pp. 271–83.

Davies, B. and R. Harré (1991), 'Positioning: The Discursive Production of Selves', *Journal for the Theory of Social Behavior*, **20** (1), pp. 43–63.

Gergen, K. (1989), 'Warranting Voice and the Elaboration of the Self', in J. Shotter and K. Gergen (eds), *Texts of Identity*, London: Sage.

Giddens, A. (1991), *Modernity and Self-Identity: Self and Society in the Late Modern Age*, Cambridge: Polity Press.

Kelly, Kevin (1999), *Ten Rules for the New Economy: 10 Radical Strategies for a Connected World*, New York: Penguin.

Kumar, K. (1995), *From Post-Industrial to Post-Modern Society: New Theories of the Contemporary World*, Oxford: Blackwell Publishers.

Law, J. (1994), *Organizing Modernity*, Oxford: Blackwell Publishers.

MacIntyre, A. (1981), *After Virtue*, London: Duckworth Press.

Salzer, M. (1994), *Identity Across Borders: A Study in the 'IKEA World'* (Linköping Studies in Management and Economics, No. 27), Linköping: Linköping University.

Shotter, J. (1989), 'Social Accountability and the Social Construction of the You', in J. Shotter and K. Gergen (eds), *Texts of Identity*. London: Sage.

Shotter, J. (1993), *Conversational Realities: Constructing Life through Language*, London: Sage.

Slugoski, B. and G. Ginsburg (1990), 'Ego Identity and Explanatory Speech', in J. Shotter, and K.J. Gergen (eds), *Texts of Identity*, London: Sage.

Weick, K. (1985), 'The Sources of Order in Unorganized Systems', in Y. Lincoln (ed.), *Themes in Recent Organizational Theory and Enquiry: The Paradigm Revolution*, London: Sage.

5. On becoming a freelance creative professional

Ellen Van Wijk and Peter Leisink

INTRODUCTION

Self-employment is no exception among professionals. In fact, many creative professionals are self-employed or work freelance. There are also many creative professionals who have regular jobs, but a majority of these have at some time considered leaving their employment in order to become self-employed.

For graphic designers, to take one category of creative professionals, self-employment is an essential characteristic of the social identity of the professional group. In the construction of the identity of graphic designers, art colleges, design journals, professional associations and informal networks play an important role (Julier 2000). As with social identities in general, the existence of this social identity depends on its continuous reproduction by the graphic designers; this, in our opinion, is not an automatic reproduction but a reflexive process in which the graphic designer makes personal choices at different stages of his or her career. These choices, at the end of art college and during the professional career, are made in private discourse with the publicly-constructed social identity; they are fed by experiences within and outside the profession, and influenced by personal appreciation of the profession and perceptions of the possibilities and constraints of self-employment.

The aim of this chapter is to gain a clearer insight into the dynamics of becoming a freelance and the role of the perception of identity in this process. By focusing the analysis on graphic designers in paid employment, it will be possible to confront the meaning which these designers give to working in an organization with the perception they have of the social identity of the graphic designer and its inherent emphasis on creative freedom and self-employment.

Theoretically, the study of graphic designers in a work organization is of interest to the study of identity creation in temporary and scattered work practices because graphic designers are employed by organizations for only short periods of time on average. The job-mobility rates for graphic designers are high; the average period of employment in an organization is only three years. Some designers leave the organization and accept jobs elsewhere, but others choose to become self-employed. What interests us is the role of the perception of the identity of graphic designers – or more generally of creative professionals – in these passages of their working life. The literature (for example Julier 2000) suggests that becoming self-employed is the outcome of a powerful professional identification, but other reasons may also be relevant, such as the desirability of life as a free agent with lucrative financial gains, or weak identification with colleagues and the organization.

Studying the process of identity construction in interaction with working life passages to a (new) job or a freelance position is also of interest because it ties in with the wider theoretical debate about the (im)possibility of constructing a coherent identity in changing and ambiguous situations in a fragmenting society (compare Bauman 1996; Sennett 1998). In this chapter, we will examine this theoretical position by questioning the existence of a stable work past as well as the static notion of identity. Based on empirical data, we will show that the construction of the identity of graphic designers is a dynamic process which finds its origin in long-standing professional ideals, and that these ideals tend to favour temporary and scattered work practices. Furthermore, we will show that for graphic designers it is (still) possible to build a coherent identity.

This chapter is organized along the following lines. First, a theoretical perspective will be sketched, in which the concepts will be elucidated. Second, the research method and context will be described. The following sections will describe and analyse empirical data on the identity construction of graphic designers who are employed, and that of freelances. The final section will present some conclusions.

THEORETICAL PERSPECTIVE

The concept of identity has received a lot of attention in recent literature. Identity refers to who we or others think we are; it defines our uniqueness as well as whom or what we belong to. Many authors in this respect differentiate between personal and social identity. Some of these authors treat identity as something that simply is (for instance Tajfel 1981). In our perspective, however, identities are not static, but produced in interactions. According to Jenkins (1996) identities are about meaning and the product of agreement and disagreement, which makes the construction of personal as well as social identities a social process; the difference between the two is the emphasis personal identity puts on difference and social identity on similarity. In this chapter we will study identity as constructed within discourses and practices which are produced within specific historical and institutional contexts (compare Giddens 1984; Fay 1996). This perspective emphasizes the dynamic process of identity construction.

We agree with Jenkins (1996, p. 4) that identity is not 'just there'; it must always be established through identification. Identification involves the extraction of cues; it is social, retrospective, and ongoing. Several of the characteristics that Weick (1995) sees as central to sense making can be recognized in this observation (Pratt 1998, p. 180). Wiley (1988, in Weick 1995, pp. 70–72) distinguishes four levels in the analysis of sense making, which in our opinion are also useful for the analysis of the identity construction of the graphic designer: (1) a personal level, (2) an interpersonal level, (3) an organizational level and (4) a symbolic level. We perceive the identity of graphic designers at the symbolic level as 'a prescription for identity construction' of the graphic designer (Czarniawska 2000, p. 273). The symbolic identity of graphic designer is constructed in the discourse about the ideal graphic designer. In our perspective, this symbolic identity does not exist without being constructed by (one of) the other levels. The personal, interpersonal and organizational levels construct their own version of the identity of graphic designer.

In this chapter, we will focus on the personal level of the identity construction of graphic designers in the context of the other levels. We are interested in how the individual identifies him- or herself with the identity of graphic designer in relation to other identities which may intrude upon the discourse on identity, such as gender or non-professional private roles such as being a musician. In addition, we are also interested in how these identification processes interact with the construction of the identity of graphic designer at the interpersonal and organizational level.

The recent attention on identity construction is based on the assumption that the construction of identity has become more problematic due to the fragmentation of society in the post-modern era. Because the individual interacts in a growing and sometimes fast-changing variety of groups, identity construction has become a 'reflexive project of connecting personal and social change' (Giddens 1991, p. 33). Authors disagree about the issue of whether under the condition of a fragmented society it is still possible for the individual to build a coherent identity. According to Giddens (1991), fragmentation does not automatically lead to multiple selves and it may just as well lead to an integrated identity. Other authors, however, suggest that due to the fragmentation of post-modern society, the individual can no longer give meaning to his or her experiences and therefore, can no longer build a coherent self (Bauman 1996; Sennett 1998).

This latter view represents an epochal perspective on identity construction, which can be challenged in two ways. First, as Elgaard Jensen and Westenholz argue in the introduction to this book, the concept of a stable work past is a problematic one. Indeed, in the case of graphic designers, Julier shows that designers have always lacked stable work practices due to competition and the need for differentiation based on the 'myth of individuated creativity' (2000, p. 36).

Secondly, we question the presupposition that a coherent identity can be constructed in a stable situation, as is supposed to have existed in the past, but not in an unstable situation. Academics still disagree on the question of whether identity construction itself has changed or that the construction of identity is more complex than was assumed before. We tend to agree with the latter perspective and assume that it is possible in an unstable situation to construct a coherent identity. On the level of self-identification, we follow Giddens, who defines identity as 'the capacity to keep a particular narrative going' (1991, p. 54). We assume that, although an individual may identify himself or herself with various identities, it is possible to blend these identities into a coherent narrative or identity. Furthermore, we assume that the part of our identity which we articulate depends on the context and whether we present it as a social or a personal identity.

THE RESEARCH

The following sections present a case study of the identity construction of creative professionals. First, the method of research and the research context will be described. The career path of creative professionals will serve as a guideline in the description of the process of the construction of the identity of graphic designers. First, attention will be given to the influence of discourses at art college. This will be followed by an exploration of the influence of experiences and discourses on the shop floor of a design studio on the way graphic designers make sense of future careers.

From a constructivist perspective, the view which creative professionals construct in an open interview is different from the view which researchers construct when they invite creative professionals to react to the constructs that they submit to them, for example, in a survey questionnaire. To do justice to this implication, this chapter presents an analysis that is based on open interviews.

The open interviews were part of an ethnographic study that was conducted for a period of three months in the autumn of 2001. One of us, Ellen Van Wijk, was present in the organization almost daily, which allowed her to make observations on the shop floor, in performance and job interviews, and also during social outings and informal meetings with employees and managers.

Interviews were held individually with eight graphic designers in a design company and one designer who had left the company to become a freelance. Based on the assumption that stories simplify the world and therefore are useful as guides for action (compare Weick 1995; Czarniawska 1998), the graphic designers were asked to narrate their educational and working careers and what they perceived to be of influence on the choices they made. All the interviews were recorded and transcribed. In these narratives, discourses or stories are constructed and reproduced according to the researcher's interpretation, and these function as sense makers in the career path of graphic designers.

The research was conducted in a design studio referred to in this chapter as One of a Kind, which is located in the centre of The Netherlands. Parallel with developments in the sector, One of a Kind has extended its services from graphic design to graphic communication and the introduction of web design. Furthermore, One of a Kind operates in a network of communication and advertising agencies and has a mix of local and internationally oriented clients.

Since its foundation by two college friends, the organization has grown into a company with 24 employees, including eight designers, which is representative of most advertising agencies, although rather large compared to other design companies (Van Wijk 2000). One of a Kind can be characterized as a professional organization with a simple structure that is managed top-down; the two founders define the strategy, give art direction, manage the office and maintain contact with the clients.

The company is established, like most agencies in the industry, in a trendy office, built in an old factory in the town centre. Behind the front office in the entrance hall, seven graphic designers share an almost open workspace on the ground floor, together with three database publishers and three web editors. Two graphic designers specialize in graphic design, and three designers in Internet design; two designers specialize in Internet as well as graphic design. This division used to be visible on the work floor as well. A glass wall separated the Internet designers from the rest, but due to a shortage of workspace, the various functions have now been combined on the shop floor. The atmosphere on the ground floor is lively, music is playing most of the time, formal and informal meetings take place and people move back and forth to the big kitchen at the rear. The kitchen is the centre of the building, where visitors wait for their appointments, people take a break, informal client meetings are held and all join for lunch. The top floor is divided into four rooms providing a place of work for the management, the project managers, and one graphic designer who prefers quieter surroundings.

One of a Kind has a young population, by age as well as by seniority. The average age of the employees is 30, which is comparable to that in other advertising agencies (Van Wijk 2000). Apart from one designer, they are all still junior designers and for three of them, One of a Kind is the first employer. Five out of the eight creative professionals have been employed at One of a Kind for less than a year. The mobility rate is high; most creative professionals at One of a Kind leave the organization within two years to start as freelances.

Generated by the expanding Internet market and several awards they received for their designs, business was flourishing at One of a Kind until the summer of 2001. During the time of the research, the effects of the collapse of the Internet market and the terrorist attack in America became visible. However, although business was slow, One of a Kind was not forced to cut down on staff, unlike other agencies in the industry. In fact, the organization still had vacancies for outstanding senior designers that turned out to be difficult to fill. According to the management, this was caused by the tendency for senior designers to start their own business and the fact that most designers were focused on Amsterdam as the capital of the design sector.

THE CONSTRUCTION OF THE IDENTITY OF GRAPHIC DESIGNERS AT ART COLLEGE

A general characteristic of the designers of One of a Kind is that they received their education at an art college. The following section will explore what discourses at art college are of influence in the construction of the identity of graphic designers.

On Becoming a Graphic Designer

Although the profession of graphic designer is not legally protected, graduation from art college as a graphic designer appears to be a powerful factor in inclusion and exclusion in the discourses and daily practices of graphic designers at One of a Kind. All designers at One of a Kind, including the founders, agree on the fact that in order to become a graphic designer, an education at an art college is required, or as one of the directors stated:

> A graphical college can teach you the technique but to become a designer you need to go to art college.

A junior web editor has an ambition to become a graphic designer, for which he feels his graduation at graphical college is sufficient. He senses, however, that he will never get the chance to become a graphic designer at One of a Kind without graduation at art college:

> Right now my job is web editing, and designing is out of the question. I like to design, you need to be an art college graduate for that. (web editor 1)

Nevertheless, he still has his hopes set on a future as a designer at One of a Kind:

> For my future here I expect the directors will let me design little things ... but to design corporate identities and things like that, that's a problem, because they only use graduated designers for that. (web editor 1)

Furthermore, observations on the shop floor showed that other employees who had also graduated from art college, but not as graphic designers, were excluded as sparring partners when designers asked for feedback.

The 'Freelance Discourse'

Apart from strict boundaries between the in- and out-group of graphic designers, differences also exist within the group of graphic designers themselves. Although all designers received their education at an art college, this education is not perceived as equal. Some art colleges have a better reputation than others, and so have their graduates. This reputation might be linked to the degree of independence that is taught at art college. The Rietveld Academy in the Netherlands, for example, has a good reputation and is known for the emphasis put on independence in art and design.

The value of 'creative freedom' appears to be a strong characteristic in the social construct of the identity of graphic designers. The construct 'creative freedom' may refer to several things:

> to be able to do your piece (designer 1)
> control over your work (designer 7)

In the interviews, several of the designers first explained why they did not choose to become free artists before they explained why they had become graphic designers. It appears that the free artist is held in higher esteem than the graphic designer, because graphic design is perceived as a more applied art form. Even though some designers express a need for 'security' as a motivation for specializing in graphic design, all designers give the same answer to the question: 'What would be a reason for leaving One of a Kind': 'the loss of "creative freedom"'.

The wish to become a freelance in the future, which many graphic designers mentioned in the interviews, appears to be linked to the value of 'creative freedom'. When asked what attracted them about being a freelance, six designers answered: 'the 'creative freedom'. We will call this the 'freelance discourse', which means that the best way to obtain total creative freedom is to become a freelance.

There are indications that the 'freelance discourse' first started to develop at art college. One of the designers mentioned:

> The Rietveld academy pushes you in a certain direction ... you are stimulated to create something unique ... actually you are trained to become self-employed ... (designer 2)

Another designer mentioned:

> 'In the first year you are taught to let go of old habits. And if you are trained at graphical college, which is very goal-oriented, it is hard to let go of all you have learned ... I consider the first year a bit of a lost year ... (designer 7)

The struggle to obtain 'creative freedom' in the sense of daring to experiment, seems to have been quite effective. In his final year, this designer and some friends decided to break free from the unwritten rule that graduates of their college end up working in big advertising agencies, and started their own business:

> In the final college year we [designer and some student friends] were discussing what to do after graduation. Our art college is actually fairly respectable, and most students find jobs in big organizations ... But we thought: 'Students from other art colleges start their own business, why doesn't that happen here, why shouldn't we start our own business?' ... During our graduation presentations we presented ourselves as a new designers collective. (designer 7)

The quotes from these designers show that the sense the designers make of the discourse is personal. Further on in the interview, designer 2 mentioned that he feels he is better off being employed in a studio, whilst designer 7 chose self-employment against the unwritten rules of his college that graduates become employed in a big advertising agency.

Two art colleges gave contradictory responses when asked whether they thought their education influenced their students with regard to the wish to become a freelance. An anonymous respondent of one academy responded in a short email:

> We have absolutely no influence on the decision-making of students whether or not they become a freelance.

In contrast, a manager of the graphic design department of another art college responded:

> I have no figures on how many of our students become a freelance after graduation ... my intuition tells me that the academy probably has its influence, but that this influence varies. Often, during his courses a student gets the idea to become a freelance or to become employed. Especially when it concerns a career as a freelance they check this idea with their teacher, who most of the time gives his

advice whether or not a student should proceed with his idea. This depends on the capacities of the student. Most teachers have their own business and know what it means to be self-employed. In most cases students get the advice to work as an employee for a couple of years, before becoming self-employed. However, recently we have seen a growing number of students starting their own business, often together with fellow students.

In the responses of the art colleges we recognize two variations of the 'freelance discourse'. In the first discourse you become a freelance of your own free will. In the second, it depends on the advice of the teacher whether or not you become a freelance. In both variants, however, we recognize the wish of prospective designers to become self-employed.

We argue that the identity of graphic designer as constructed by the designers who were interviewed, involves two prominent characteristics, namely the value of 'professional, creative products' and of 'creative freedom'. These examples show the contribution of art colleges' discourse to the construction of the identity of the graphic designer in two ways: (1) a specialized education at art college turns you into a member of the group of professional graphic designers; and (2) 'creative freedom' represents the highest value, and to this end the 'freelance discourse' points the way. The teachers at the art academy, who are self-employed designers themselves, enact the social structure of graphic design in which 'creative freedom' and freelancing are connected.

Julier's analysis (2000) of the culture of design provides further insights that help to understand why and how art schools perform a role in the 'freelance discourse'. Throughout history, designers have been struggling with the status of their activities and striving for recognition of their profession as an art form. As an outcome of this struggle, creative potential is the driving principle in art schools, in the selection of new students and the (lack of) organization of the curriculum. The emphasis is on individual creativity. Because of this, art schools have always resisted state attempts to make art and design education more vocational and compliant with the formal regulations which prevail in the educational system. According to Julier (2000, p. 36) it is also the 'myth of individuated creativity' inherited from art education, on which designers draw to differentiate themselves from each other. (Of course, creating a distinctive creative profile is also a means of competing with each other for clients' interest (Julier 2000, p. 37)) Thus individual creativity and absence of formal procedures are established from the beginning as inherent features of the social identity of creative professionals and are continually reproduced in art college.

In the Netherlands, the 'freelance discourse' has become institutionalized in the starter's stipendium. This is a financial donation that is granted for promising business plans, and is meant to give designers who start their own business the financial freedom to develop their skills further and build a fruitful network in their first year. Designers can apply for this stipendium within two and a half years after graduation.

Although these examples show that art colleges have a major influence on the identity construction of graphic designers, this influence is not deterministic. We found first indications that in their determination of whether or not to become a freelance, the graphic designers make their own decisions, based on social and personal cues, perceiving these cues on the one hand as possibilities and on the other hand as barriers.

GRAPHIC DESIGNERS AT ONE OF A KIND

After graduation, the creative professional has the option of becoming a freelance or an employee. In the social construction of the identity of the graphic designer, becoming a freelance seems the ultimate way to obtain 'creative freedom'. However, all designers in this study opted for employment, although two designers combined this employment with a career as a freelance and one designer recently started as a full-time freelance. In the following sections we will explore why these graphic designers chose to accept employment at One of a Kind, and which discourses are of influence in the sense-making process regarding future careers.

The 'Professional Community Discourse'

Various cues were mentioned by the graphic designers as reasons why they had applied for a job at One of a Kind. The thing that all designers mentioned was that they could identify themselves with the work there. The following quotes are applicable to all designers:

> I found some sort of kinship with what I did at the academy ... the way things are designed, how you present or develop certain ideas. Some sort of directness, some sort of feeling. (designer 8)

> The work they produce is quite lively, or varied ... and that is something that attracts me as well, the fun, or liveliness of the work, you see many different things ... and I pictured myself working there. (designer 3)

However, this was not the main reason for applying for all designers. The two part-time designers who were also part-time freelances applied because they could work part-time at One of a Kind.

> Actually it [the application] was a pure coincidence ... at a certain moment my art

college sent me this advertisement ... and I thought: Ok it is part-time and that I found important ... and it was the Internet and I liked that as well. (designer 4)

And then to my surprise the advertisement said that the studio were also looking for part-timers which I had seen nowhere else, and I thought that it could be interesting. (designer 7)

Apart from the possibility of working part-time, designer 4 also mentioned the attractiveness of the Internet as a reason. Five other designers also mentioned the possibility of designing web pages or a combination of graphic and Internet design as a reason for applying to One of a Kind.

Furthermore, seven of the designers considered One of a Kind to be a 'good learning environment', although only two designers mentioned it as a reason for applying for a job. Four designers mentioned the reputation of One of a Kind as a reason for applying for a job:

It [One of a Kind] has a good name ... One of a Kind is well known in the world of designers ... So yes, it has always been a studio where I wanted to work. (designer 3)

Over the years, One of a Kind has won several awards with graphical as well as web designs, which is why they have made a name for themselves in the designer world. The reputation of One of a Kind seems linked to the perception of it as a good learning environment. However, not all designers are attracted to the fame of One of a Kind. Two designers had their doubts whether they should apply for a job there because they feared the company was too trendy:

You hear those stories about those boys of One of a Kind, that they are so arrogant ... and One of a Kind thinks itself one of the best ... One of a Kind seemed to me a very trendy company and I thought I'm not like that. But they offered me what I wanted, so I thought I'll try it anyway. (designer 9)

The final characteristic that was mentioned is the atmosphere of the organization. Although only three designers mentioned atmosphere as an important reason for applying for a job at One of a Kind, all designers said it was an important reason why they enjoyed working there. The designers used the word 'atmosphere' in two different ways. The first way referred to the informal style in which the work process is organized. All designers stated that they would leave the organization:

[I]f it turns into a big advertising agency. (designer 1)

A 'big advertising agency' stands for an organization in which processes are standardized too much, but it also refers to the designing of corporate identities, which in their perception is the main product of big companies. To them, this type of organization represents the loss of 'creative freedom', or as one designer mentioned:

> Most students work for big companies, designing corporate identities, it seems they're good at listening and keeping their mouths shut. (designer 7)

The other meaning of 'atmosphere' refers to contacts with other colleagues. All designers appreciated the informal contacts on the shop floor and some designers mentioned friendships with other colleagues. However, the value of 'creative freedom' has its impact on the interaction with colleagues. In an art direction meeting with all designers, it was mentioned that:

> The creative process and its outcome are personal and an ego-thing, this makes cooperation with other designers problematic unless it concerns a complex project. (designer 2)

In general, however, most designers mentioned one or two colleagues that were valuable as sparring partners for them.

In these characteristics we recognize what we will call 'professional community discourse'. This refers to the way the designers, as well as the management, promote the advantages of being employed at One of a Kind. The professional community stands for a warm, safe haven in which the professional is invited to develop his or her own talents. In the 'professional community discourse' at One of a Kind, several themes can be observed: (1) One of a Kind offers interesting accounts and products which give room for 'creative freedom', (2) It is a good learning environment, (3) career prospects and income security are offered, and (4) One of a Kind feels like a home.

The 'professional community discourse' shows the influence of other discourses. It reflects the importance of a distinctive creative profile as mentioned before, and the value of creative freedom, in which we recognize the influence of art college. Furthermore, the 'professional community discourse' at One of a Kind appears to fit the 'freelance discourse' as expressed by one of the art colleges: first you accept a job to become more experienced, and then you may start your own business. The management is convinced that One of a Kind offers good career opportunities for designers, but one of them also expressed:

> For the development of outstanding designers it is probably best to become a freelance. (manager 1)

Here we recognize the 'freelance discourse', which shows that its influence is so powerful that it is even enacted by managers of creative organizations. However, the 'professional community discourse' as enacted by the management also reflects the evolution of employment at One of a Kind, as a result of the learning process of the founders:

> The first person we ever cooperated with after the foundation of One of a Kind, a project manager, was immediately made partner. But after a year he left, which gave an awful lot of paperwork with buy-outs and everything. Then we decided not to do this anymore. New employees have to work for a couple of years before we decide whether or not they can become partners.

And:

> In the beginning we welcomed every new employee as an equal member of One of a Kind. But of course this is not the case. You want to be equal but you're not: There are two bosses and an employee, and you cannot expect someone to take full responsibility for something that is not his or hers. (manager 2)

In an informal conversation, the other manager mentioned:

> Although we keep looking for senior designers or an art director we know that it is difficult to find one that will fit in at One of a Kind. It is difficult to mould an experienced designer into the concept of One of a Kind and when the designer would fit in he or she is more interested in starting his or her own business. Designers who have just graduated from art college are easier to mould. (manager 1)

These quotes show that it has not always been the intention of the management to be a learning environment. Furthermore, they show how the management makes sense of the tension between the value of 'creative freedom' and the restrictions of the organization. The importance of a warm social atmosphere seems to be a relic of earlier times, when the studio was still small and employees were perceived as equals, although at this point the management is struggling with the question of how to become more professional without losing the informal atmosphere.

> A while ago I found there was a lack of professionalism. There was more humour than the work that was produced justified. It is a difficult topic, when I mention it the other manager will say it belongs to One of a Kind. (manager 2)

Discourses on Future Careers

When asked whether they still enjoyed working at One of a Kind after having been employed for some time, all designers said they did and nobody mentioned concrete plans to leave. Forcing the designers to think about their future career plans might seem premature. However, previous research (Van

Wijk 2000) showed that 87 per cent of the creative professionals had considered looking for a new job. The same was found at One of a Kind. Although nobody expressed concrete plans, seven designers considered staying there for one or two years as already quite a long period. An example of this was found the moment one of the designers received her new and very expensive laptop, which she was able to buy because of a PC scheme that One of a Kind offered employees. This scheme is a tax facility in which the company lends you the money for a computer, which is paid back in instalments from your salary. All designers stood around the designer and admired the computer. Several designers mentioned that they were now considering entering the PC scheme as well. A jocular remark that this was the ultimate way to commit employees to the company, spurred the designer who had bought the computer to respond:

> Oh no, I've arranged that I pay the computer back in one year, and if necessary I'll pay my debts in cash if I want to leave before that. (designer 3)

Over time, a shift in the appreciation of the characteristics of One of a Kind can be observed. Once the graphic designers have created their own products, it seems they perceive a feeling of equality with the art directors, or as two designers mentioned:

> Well, my whole view of the company changed. I discovered that, eh at that time I looked up to One of a Kind ... but now I see that I'm a part of the company, that I have those qualities myself. (designer 1)

> I've thought about it for a long time, but I don't want to have anyone above me anymore, I only want someone standing next to me and that is what's happening more and more. (designer 2)

Another aspect of this shift is that designers seem to perceive fewer learning opportunities. At this point, most designers get restless in their jobs. Most designers start considering future careers and eight designers considered freelancing as an option.

Three discourses can be observed in making sense of future careers: (1) the 'freelance discourse', (2) the 'professional community discourse', and (3) discourses of other identities. For analytical purposes, the discourses will be examined here separately, but in the interviews the graphic designers expressed a mixture of these discourses.

The 'Freelance Discourse'

The main discourse that can be observed at One of a Kind when it comes to future careers is the 'freelance discourse'. In its pure form it is found with the designer who recently left the organization to become a freelance.

After graduation this graphic designer already had vague plans to become self-employed, but she also made some unsolicited applications. In the meantime, 'out of a need for security', this graphic designer remained employed in the organization in which she had done her practical placement. After a couple of months, One of a Kind responded to her application and offered her a job as graphic and Internet designer. She had her doubts about taking the job because she felt that One of a Kind might be too trendy. Furthermore, she still had plans to start her own business. However, the combination of Internet and graphical design that One of a Kind offered her, made her decide to try the job for a period of six months. She ended up working at One of a Kind for a period of two years:

> I was afraid to commit myself, but once I started at One of a Kind it turned out that it was a nice organization to work for ... and that the colleagues were very kind ... I got nice projects and was able to make a CD-Rom. (designer 9)

In the second year of her employment this graphic designer suffered from repetitive RSI, which forced her to think about her career again. The projects she did at One of a Kind had become less interesting and she felt a lack of creative freedom. She felt that freelancing would offer her more creative freedom and more variation in her work and she decided to apply for a starter's stipendium. At the same time, she also applied for a job at a small company that former colleagues of One of a Kind had started. This company offered her attractive Internet projects, nice colleagues, and she would have more variety and responsibility in her work because of the small size of the company.

> In a big organization you are just a cog in the machine, and some tasks you don't do yourself anymore. I felt that the only thing I did was to sit at the computer all day, while I like what I do now: calling printers and visiting clients. (designer 9)

To her own surprise, however, she was granted a starter's stipendium. She decided to take her chance and start her own business and turned down the job that was offered to her.

The interview took place seven months after the graphic designer started as a freelance. When asked what was so attractive to her about being a freelance she mentioned:

> I have had this since I was at high school, this need for freedom. I always hated the idea to work from nine to five. It seemed like a prison to me ... but then I started working and I found out that it didn't feel that way. But I decided to become a freelance to gain more creative freedom ... not that One of a Kind repressed my

creative freedom but it is some sort of ego, the wish to put your own name on your work. Actually it is feeling that you did it yourself. (designer 9)

She had to admit that the freedom she thought she would gain had some negative side effects. First, she missed her colleagues – an aspect of freelancing she had never considered before – not only for company but also for feedback:

And then you start and find out that it is hard to be on your own. You lack any form of feedback ... but I still feel it is better to be a freelance, although I miss my colleagues very much. (designer 9)

She had always hoped she would meet a partner to start a business with, but unfortunately this had not happened. The other designer she was sharing a studio with had different office hours and she did not know anybody else she trusted sufficiently to be a partner.

Second, she found out that 'creative freedom' is sometimes an illusion when you are still building a network:

I should use this year to do the things I want to do and develop myself, and to build a client file. Nevertheless, it is difficult because sometimes you think you should not make business cards, but on the other hand next year I won't have a stipendium and maybe this assignment is useful for my client file. (designer 9)

This hesitation about turning down uninteresting accounts seems grounded in a lack of skills to bring in new customers, which seems a 'horrifying' task to her. Another negative effect of being a freelance are the longer working hours she now has to undertake, although she admitted she also liked the longer hours. Notwithstanding the negative elements of being a freelance, a return to employment seems out of the question:

If I had to choose I would choose for what I am doing now, but I would prefer to do it together with lots of colleagues. (designer 9)

The interview shows that the wish to become a freelance develops dynamically. At first the wish seems based on a need for flexible working hours, but the actual step of applying for a starter's stipendium is based on the need for 'creative freedom'. Furthermore, the data show that the step of becoming a freelance is situational. The possibilities and constraints that the graphic designer perceives are of influence in the decision-making process. In this case, the graphic designer might still have been employed, had not a starter's stipendium been granted to her.

A retrospective element can be found in the appreciation of colleagues, because only after the designer had left One of a Kind, did she start to think about the added value of colleagues. This is an element of the 'professional community discourse'. It seems that the 'professional community discourse' and the 'freelance discourse' intermingle and create some sort of a dilemma between the values of 'creative freedom' and feedback from colleagues.

Confirmation of this dilemma is to be found in the outcomes of a survey of self-employed graphic designers in the Netherlands (Puffelen and Schumacher 1991). Although some designers admitted that they could benefit from working with colleagues, especially when it comes to feedback, the perceived loss of their autonomy and 'creative freedom' prevented them from doing so. However, three out of four designers felt that it was important to have the possibility of cooperating with other designers. Indeed, all graphic designers employed by One of a Kind who considered concrete freelance activities or plans preferred to cooperate with other designers.

The biggest problem that self-employed graphic designers perceive was a lack of the skill of bringing in new clients and an aversion towards it. Another survey showed that the self-employed perceived a significantly higher autonomy, but the long working hours and the financial insecurity were regarded as disadvantages of being self-employed (Smulders and Evers 2000).

At One of a Kind, variations on the 'freelance discourse' can be found which seem to be an outcome, on the one hand, of the perceived 'creative freedom' while being employed, and on the other hand of the perceived difficulties of being a freelance. The first variant we will call the 'part-time freelance discourse', the second we call the 'on becoming a freelance discourse'.

The 'part-time freelance discourse' is reflected by three designers, and already brought into practice by two of them. One designer mentioned the economic recession as a reason for postponing the step to freelancing, although at the same time he considered the starter's stipendium to be an attractive impulse to start his own business, and while time is running out for him he has to make a decision soon. He has built a sort of safety net into his future career plans:

> The ideal situation would be ... suppose I get the starter's stipendium then maybe I could work three days at One of a Kind and two days on an individual [music] project ... Some things are very well arranged here ... It also has to do with the economic recession ... Recently I heard all these stories of studios that had to fire their people ... I'm happy that I have a good job and don't need to worry about a thing. (designer 6)

A part-time freelance mentioned:

> Being able to say no to an assignment gives you a feeling of power. Of course this is only possible because of my steady income at One of a Kind. (designer 7)

Although these designers expressed a feeling that freelancing meant more 'creative freedom' than was offered to them by One of a Kind, they all preferred the option of a combination of employment and freelancing. Having a stable income was mentioned as the main cue for not wanting to become a full-time freelance yet; a stable income would help to obtain 'creative freedom' whilst freelancing.

Six designers reflected the 'on becoming a freelance discourse'. The following quotes are applicable to all six:

> I won't leave One of a Kind for another studio ... If there is a step after One of a Kind it will be starting my own business, alone or with friends. This would be when I stop learning, that is very important to me ... I think the main reason why I would leave would be taking away my 'creative freedom'. (designer 1)

> I have a good opportunity for personal development here. I have a good feeling about it ... for now, I don't have the intention to become a freelance. (designer 8)

In the interviews these designers mentioned that they perceived enough learning possibilities and 'creative freedom' inside the organization, but being a freelance in the future seemed a reasonable option. Various possible reasons were given for leaving the organization, but all six mentioned a lack of learning opportunities and the loss of 'creative freedom' as main cues in making the decision on when to become a freelance.

The 'Professional Community Discourse'

This discourse shows two varieties, which seem to be based on the perceived opportunities outside the organization. The first version is reflected by the only senior designer at One of a Kind. As reason for applying for a job there, he mentioned that when he first saw the work:

> I felt some kind of infatuation, like, this is what I want, maybe I want to work there. (designer 2)

Furthermore, he mentioned a strong identification with the management. At the time of the interview he was at a turning point in his career. In a performance interview he expressed that he felt it was time to settle down and buy a nice house, and also:

> I have worked for a long time at the studio and have an important influence on the work of One of a Kind. I would like to be more involved in One of a Kind ... But now it is your studio and my name is nowhere to be found. (designer 2)

While he perceived a lack of capacity for becoming a freelance as well as a lack of other interesting studios to work for, a logical step would be to become a partner at One of a Kind. He had thought about such a proposal and decided that he wanted to combine the positive aspects of being employed and being a freelance:

> I want to be a sort of shop in shop at One of a Kind. This studio is more of a facilitating company. (designer 2)

Nevertheless, he still nourished the dream of starting his own business one day:

> Maybe I am now developing myself so that in the future I can become self-employed, just as the Rietveld academy taught us to. (designer 2)

In this version of the 'professional community discourse', the lack of possibilities outside the organization seems to be the main cue in the process of decision-making. Considering the fact that the dream of starting as a freelance is still there, this story might even suggest that the identification with the product and the management he expressed in the interview was a result of this lack of possibilities, and an example of sense making driven by plausibility rather than accuracy (Weick, 1995).

The second version of the 'professional community discourse' is expressed by another designer and seems based on a more genuine identification with the organization. One designer for whom One of a Kind was the first employer was keeping open the option of one day becoming a freelance, but at the same time, after a meeting in which the first outcomes of this study were discussed with all employees of One of a Kind, he mentioned:

> I keep saying that I intend to leave One of a Kind one day, it is not cool to say you want to stay here, but deep down inside I have to admit I like it here a lot and I can imagine myself being a partner of One of a Kind one day. (designer 1)

This designer perceived possibilities inside as well as outside the organization. His identification with the products and the management seems based on a perceived similarity between his identity as a graphic designer and the image of the organization, which might lead to an internalization of the values and norms of the organization.

Discourses of Other Identities

The 'freelance discourse' and the 'professional community discourse' are based on future careers as a graphic designer. Five designers were not sure whether their future career would be in graphic design. One designer mentioned:

> And then my dream was to work at a famous Dutch design studio. And now, what shall I think of now? (designer 3)

But when asked whether freelancing would be an option, the same designer mentioned:

> Maybe it would be, but right now I'm more focused on what I want to do in life in general. (designer 3)

Moreover, another designer stated:

> I discovered that I like teaching something to people ... for example painting or drawing. I would like doing that. But I also like photography. (designer 5)

And:

> Right now I'm thinking about what I want, I have the age to think about my future, do I want to live together with my partner, do I want children. (designer 5)

Exploring interests outside graphic design like film, music or photography could be a possibility, but also a balance between a career and private life was taken into consideration: things designers did not find the time for now or they felt one should not be interested in as a graphic designer. Being a graphic designer seemed to be a way of life in the perception of these people. The following quote represents the various replies the designers gave to the question of whether they perceived themselves to be true designers:

> For me graphic design is the best job in the world ... but I'm not the type that organizes her whole life around it. (designer 9)

Most of the time this answer was followed by an example of a famous graphic designer who, in their perception, represented a true graphic designer.

For most designers, identification with One of a Kind seemed to be situational and based on a perceived similarity between the identity of graphic designer and the image of the organization. In the early stages of their employment, the perceived possibilities for personal development, as expressed in the 'professional community discourse', appeared to be the strongest cue for getting and remaining in employment. After some time the designers perceived their position in the organization as more equal to that of the management and the learning aspect as a less salient characteristic of the image of the organization; then the influence of the 'freelance discourse' appeared to become stronger. This might be an outcome of the 'freelance discourse' as the teachers at art college enacted it as we saw above: first you accept employment to become more experienced and then you may start your own business.

The 'freelance discourse' appeared to be dominant in the decision-making relating to future careers: a major theme in the process seemed to be the (dis)similarity of the image of the organization as perceived by the designers and their perception of the graphic designer, especially when it came to 'creative freedom'. A mixture of cues appeared to have its influence on the sense-making process. The designers sometimes indicated that similar cues were important; however, in their decision-making about whether to stay at One of a Kind or become a freelance they give a personal interpretation of these social, organizational and personal cues, perceiving them on the one hand as possibilities and on the other hand as barriers. This confirms Weick's observation that sense-making is an individual process 'in the sense that structures contained within individual minds are imposed on streams of individual elapsed experience that are capable of an infinite number of individual reconstructions' (2001, p. 202). The 'professional community discourse' and discourses of other identities seem to play a more ambiguous role. On the one hand they may help to make sense of future careers, but on the other hand they can also conflict with the future suggested by the freelance discourse.

CONCLUSION

Can we learn from this study of graphic designers about life and identity construction in temporary and scattered work practices? This is a relevant question to start with, because many studies on identity formation in the network age focus on temporary and scattered work practices, while the organization in which this research was conducted can be typified as a traditional organization with a simple structure in which the creative professionals have a permanent employment contract. However, this study shows that, at least in the case of graphic designers, there is a sliding scale between stable employment and temporary and scattered work practices, if only in the sense that job mobility is so high as to make work temporary. More importantly, employment may formally be stable, but the graphic designers make sense of their lives and enact their choices within a discourse which emphasizes 'creative freedom' and they make distinctions which are believed to be predicated on self-employment. We argue that this yearning for independence might be better explained by long-standing professional ideals than by 'post-modern changes' in society.

What emerges from this case study is that the process of identity construction has a recursive and ongoing character. Creative professionals perceive their creativity as a personal characteristic on which they base their initial decision to go to art college, while especially art college and, in the case of some designers, the design studio, appear subsequently to be of influence on their construction of the identity of graphic designer. This influence is not deterministic in the sense of occurring without the agency of the (prospective) designer. The data show that the designers appropriate the art college's discourse on 'creative freedom' and enact their individual decisions based on the sense they make of social, organizational and personal cues.

Indications were found that various conflicting identities appeared to play a role at several stages in the process of the construction of the identity of graphic designer. A conflict was found between the need for 'creative freedom', one of the main characteristics of the identity of graphic designer, and the identity of employee at One of a Kind. In the process of making sense of this conflict, the perceived image of the organization, other identities, personal characteristics and contextual factors appear to be of influence, thereby illustrating the theoretical assumption that within a specific historical and institutional context, multiple and sometimes conflicting identities lay the foundations for identification – with the profession and/or with the design studio and/or other foci – and that identification is the process in which new identities may arise. Depending on the perceived constraints and possibilities, the solution to this ambiguity that is most favoured by the designers is actually to become a freelance.

REFERENCES

Bauman, Z. (1996), 'From Pilgrim to Tourist', in S. Hall and P. du Gay (eds), *Questions of Cultural Identity*, London, UK and Thousand Oaks, US: Sage, pp. 18–36.

Czarniawska, B. (1998), *A Narrative Approach to Organization Studies*, London, UK and Thousand Oaks, US: Sage.

Czarniawska, B. (2000), 'Identity Lost or Identity Found?', in M. Schultz, M.J. Hatch and M. Holten Larsen (eds), *The Expressive Organization*, Oxford, UK and New York: Oxford University Press, pp. 271–83.

Fay, B. (1996), *Contemporary Philosophy of Social Science*, Oxford, UK and Malden, US: Blackwell Publishers Ltd.

Giddens, A. (1984), *The Constitution of Society*, Cambridge: Polity Press.

Giddens, A. (1991), *Modernity and Self-identity*, Cambridge: Polity Press.

Jenkins, R. (1996), *Social Identity*, London, UK and New York, US: Routledge.

Julier, G. (2000), *The Culture of Design*, London, UK and Thousand Oaks, US: Sage.

Pratt, M.G. (1998), 'To Be or Not to Be? Central Questions in Organizational Identification', in D.A. Whetten and P.C. Godfrey (eds), *Identity in Organizations: Building Theory Through Conversations*, London, UK and Thousand Oaks, US: Sage, pp. 171–207.

Puffelen, F. van and B. Schumacher (1991), *Ontwerpers, Ontwerpbureaus en hun*

Opdrachtgevers, Amsterdam: SEO.
Sennett, R. (1998), *The Corrosion of Character*, London, UK and New York, US: W.W. Norton & Company.
Smulders, P.G.W. and G.E. Evers (2000), 'Wie Wordt Zelfstandige en Wie Werknemer en Wat Zijn de Effecten?', *Tijdschrift voor Arbeidsvraagstukken*, **16** (4), 320–34.
Tajfel, H. (1981), *Human Groups and Social Categories: Studies in Social Psychology*, New York: Cambridge University Press.
Van Wijk, E. (2000), *Arbeidsbeleving bij Communicatie-Adviesbureaus 2000*, Amsterdam: VEA.
Weick, K.E. (1995), *Sensemaking in Organizations*, London, UK and Thousand Oaks, US: Sage.
Weick, K.E. (2001), *Making Sense of the Organization*, Oxford, UK and Malden, US: Blackwell Publishers.

6. Emerging identities beyond organizational boundaries

Ann Westenholz

THE RESEARCH AGENDA

In *The Corrosion of Character*, Richard Sennett (1998) argues that, as a consequence of the endless changes caused by the new 'flexible capitalism', individuals are increasingly losing their bearings and finding it difficult to orient themselves. A sense of meaninglessness is growing, and the individual's character (loyalty and mutual commitment, pursuit of long-term goals and delayed gratification for the sake of a future end) is corroding as a consequence of the instability of, for instance, work relations in networks and teams. He further argues that social bonds and dependencies are sustaining 'character' (or in my terminology, 'identity'). It is clear that Sennett thus disagrees with the way in which the management literature pays homage to the independence of the Free Agent and to the potentials of flexible business processes. He stresses that the outcome of flexible capitalism is not freedom but confusion, fear, and meaninglessness. The individual is no longer able to construct anticipatory stories about the future. It is no longer possible to evoke through speech a meaningful 'we' in the stories.

Sennett's analysis is interesting, not only because it has attracted so much attention in the social discourse, but also because his basic analysis refutes the image of 'the atomic individual' underlying the concept of the Free Agent. Instead he argues, as I do, for a social psychological understanding of the individual in which identities grow from relationships among individuals, relationships that also work to sustain and change identities (Emirbayer 1997; Gergen 1994, 1999, 2001). This homage paid to Sennett's works is important, because I challenge his conception of the character as melting down to, among other things, networks and teamwork.

It appears to me that Sennett, in his reasoning, treats stability and flexibility one-dimensionally. By viewing the problem from this one-dimensional perspective, he inextricably intertwines two dimensions that should be viewed as separate. One dimension concerns the extent to which the human condition is stable or flexible. The other dimension concerns the extent to which the individual relates, if at all, to his or her environments. By merging the two dimensions, Sennett neglects the possibility of living a meaningful, relational life in a flexible world.

This criticism can be expressed in another way, by distinguishing between an ontological and an empirical level in the analysis. Stability and flexibility in work relationships belong to the empirical level, whereas the idea of humans as relational relates to the ontological level. According to this reasoning, people in flexible situations also relate to the context in which they find themselves. How this takes place is an empirical question.

I want to challenge Sennett's assumption by analysing identity stories from the IT field and their impact on and transformation of identities in work practices that characterize the flexible economy: temporary and scattered project work within IT software development. Based on concrete IT practices, I analyse the ways in which identities unfold in these flexible practices – an unfolding which does not point unequivocally towards the individuals being left alone in a chaotic world without direction and in which they are necessarily put out of action.

In my view, 'identity' is socially constructed stories about individuals and their surroundings as they engage in their work practices. These stories position the individual 'in practice', in that they are tied to certain 'subject positions' – at the same time as the stories call into existence the individuals as subjects who are acting in certain ways. Identities are socially constructed phenomena that simultaneously help people feel secure and enable them to act. Identities are not, however, static. In practice they are socially negotiated, and in the process the delineation between the individual and his or her environment changes. This understanding of identities is close to that of Hall (1996, pp. 5–6), when he writes: 'I refer to "identities" as a meeting place of discourses and practices that attempt to "make us toe the line" as social subjects of particular discourses, and of subjectivity producing processes that construct us as subjects that can be "evoked through speech"'. (See also Ezzy 1998; Davies and Harré 1990).

In stories about the individual's identity, I search for accounts about delineation of and relations between the individuals and their surroundings. I argue that identity stories hold a description of the individual as a subject – a 'me' – in relation to two different environments. The 'me' of the subject is often described in relation to other subjects – the 'you' – and the two phenomena 'me' and 'you' assume the status of a common subject – the 'us' – acting jointly. Often, in these stories, the subject is also described in relation to another type of environment – an assumed objective environment called 'it'. This relationship expresses the alienation of the subject in the face of an environment towards which the subject acts instrumentally.

Whether or not the stories encompass these relationships is an empirical question. Certain stories may not present the concepts 'me', 'you', 'us' and 'it', and the relationships may not be evoked through speech in the story. Therefore, it is possible to imagine various types of identity stories in which the elements and their interrelationships are evoked through speech of varying intensity. Like other concepts, identity stories as an analytical tool are socially constructed; and in relation to my analysis, the fertility of the concept depends on the degree to which the concepts and the relationships are recognizable in the social field under analysis.

In relation to the following analysis, it is important to distinguish between *practice stories* and *field stories*. Practice stories are about identities that are evoked through speech during work practice and which tell something about the identities involved in those practices. Field stories, on the other hand, are identity stories that have been widely distributed and are distinguishable in a social field without the storytellers necessarily recognizing themselves in the stories.

In the analysis, I attempt to understand how identities are negotiated in temporary and scattered work practice through the social processes of meaning creation, which – I argue – takes place in meaning arenas.

I consider work practice to be a reification (for example a social construction on which consensus exists) which involved individuals use to describe what they are doing when engaged in, for example, developing and adapting IT software products.

In keeping with Weick (1995, p. 17), I understand meaning creation to be a probability-driven continuous social construction process embedded in the identity construction in which sensible environments enact. The process is often retrospective and involves a focus on extracted cues, which are simple, familiar structures. Weick (1995, pp. 49–55) compares these structures with 'seeds' from which we develop a larger meaning of what is happening. In using the term 'seeds', Weick claims that meaning creation has an open-ended dual quality because, like seeds, structures delimit the outcome (not everything can happen). On the other hand, the seeds are not determining the concrete outcome of actions that are developed in interaction between the seeds and their environments. It is my assumption that the field identity stories function as seeds in the processes of meaning creation.

I argue that meaning creation takes place at a *meaning arena*. This is formed around issues or fractures emerging in work practice. These issues give rise to 'actors' with different and sometimes opposing identities and interpretation of the issues. The actors may not all participate in the work practice and they may not all have an impact on the social construction of meaning, but they try to negotiate an understanding of what is going on and by so doing identities might change. Meaning arenas are dynamic as actors enter and leave.

Actors are, like work practice, a reification: a social construction on which consensus exists in the sense that we agree on drawing boundaries around a unit named an 'actor'. Actors might be individuals, groups, organizations and so on. Identities are then negotiated around issues or fractures emerging in work practice as actors make sense, drawing on and transforming field identity stories. The traditional analytical distinction between micro and macro phenomena collapses in the analysis. It is only in work practice that widely distributed field stories (some may call them macro phenomena) play a role in meaning creation (which some may call micro phenomena). Simultaneously, in work practice, the actors in the meaning creation transform field identity stories in the negotiation of identities.

RESEARCH DESIGN[1]

The research design is constructed around three methodological approaches: 1) visits to concrete work practices, 2) travels through the IT field, and 3) the study of documents.

Visits to Practice

One of the central goals in choosing the research design was to get close to the social work practice in order to observe and interview IT people working in networks and teams. The temporary and scattered nature of this work was somewhat of a challenge to my own daily work practice, because it required me to follow IT workers across company boundaries and to fit the visits into my other obligations. I visited two IT companies several times during 2000 and 2001 and spent several days observing and talking with IT workers – often several times. I was able to type my observations immediately on my laptop without disturbing anyone; all the others were glued to their screens. During the course of the study, some of the employees worked in other companies where I visited them, or, if that were impossible, I came to their homes in the evening. Furthermore, some of the staff worked with employees from other companies, from whom they were geographically separated, and I visited them wherever they were. In some cases the work practice I was following ceased to exist before I was able to revisit, and I would either have to abandon that practice or content myself with retrospective interviews.

A Voyage through the IT Field

A second step was to design an electronic questionnaire. The challenge was that I did not immediately know how to contact respondents, many of the IT workers being scattered, in temporary places, not employed in companies, or not union members. Some IT workers spend the majority of their working hours in the field or working with people external to the company. In the autumn of 2001 I embarked upon what later proved to be an immense networking activity, tracing information about the flexible, boundary-transgressing IT workers and how to contact them. The purpose of this exercise was to find IT people embedded in large-scale networks who knew where to find the relevant IT respondents. During this process, the electronic questionnaire provided a brilliant opportunity to talk with 'large spiders' in the web that represents the institutional Danish IT field: managers of IT agencies and net portals that mediate contact between companies looking for temporary labour and IT people looking for temporary work; managers of companies offering training programmes for IT workers; and professional independent IT consultants with large networks. One contact would direct me to other contacts, and I was able not only to question these people about relevant questionnaire respondents, but was able to interview them about their daily practices as actors in the IT field.[2] (The answers from the electronic questionnaire do not play a role in the analysis in this chapter.)

A Study of Documents

The third data source for the study took the form of documentary Internet material about various associations and companies, as well as a series of books describing and interpreting events in the development of IT products.

In this chapter I draw primarily on the qualitative data, consisting of a 65-page logbook, 45 interviews transcribed to 1000 pages, and the documentary material. I am not claiming that the data are representative of the IT field. Neither do I find the requirement of representativeness meaningful in relation to a field where boundaries are not clearly delimited. But I do claim that the data is rich in relation to the concrete work practices analysed.

I begin by describing field stories – some would call them discourses – about identity as an IT worker. I have drawn on the documentary material and interviews during my journey through the IT field. After presenting the field identity stories, I describe certain examples that in various ways illustrate the daily practice and meaning creation related to the formation of networks and teams within which the IT software is developed. Here I draw on my visits to the workplaces. Although my data are taken directly from my research, I have changed names, places, and products.

FOUR FIELD IDENTITY STORIES OF THE IT WORKER

On my tour through the IT field, I encountered four widely known (although not necessarily widely accepted) understandings of what it implies to be an IT worker. In this context I do not discuss the way in which the four stories are socially constructed, how they have travelled and get transformed through the IT field, or whether variations of the stories exist. Instead I present the field stories as empirical phenomena that represent – I argue – the baggage on which actors draw in negotiating identities in their concrete work practices. But before discussing these negotiations in and about practice, I describe the four stories under the headings:

- Citizen in the Company
- Free Agent in the Market
- Open-Source Grassrooter
- Project Maker in a Professional Community

The Field Story of the 'Citizen in the Company'

The field story of the Citizen in the Company is the story of a relationship between an individual employee and a company. It is a story of ownership, not necessarily in the sense of capital ownership, but as a participant in decision processes in the company and as a holder of intellectual capital. The 'new employee' is involved in decisions about the daily work and in the company's long-term strategic decisions – the latter through representatives. The Citizen in the Company is not only a phenomenon that produces 'glue' in flexible companies; it also gives meaning to the life of the individual during a time when other identities (for example national) are losing ground. The company comes to represent the arena in which meaningful work and social life meet (Flecker and Hofbauer 1998, p. 111; Miller and Rose 1995; Christensen and Westenholz 1999).

The Field Story of the 'Free Agent in the Market'

The field story about the Free Agent pays homage to the freedom achieved by the individual who operates independently in the market rather than depending on permanent long-term employment in a company (see for example Aley 1995; Bridges 1994; Budtz and Moseholm 2000; Mandag Morgen 1999; Pink 2001; Stokholm 2001). Such freedom can wear many faces.

A Free Agent can avoid involvement in heavy decision processes, irritating rules, and the constraining division of work that characterizes life as an employee in a company. Depending on their market value, Free Agents can fly from flower to flower, optimizing their self-actualization. The highly competent IT person whose market value is high would probably find life as a Free Agent to be preferable. A second advantage of the life of a Free Agent is the ability to alternate between work, family and other types of activities in a much more flexible way than can an ordinary employee, taking the kids to kindergarten and picking them up again, taking holidays when the timing best suits finances and private life. The Free Agent can live in exotic localities and work via the Internet. Third, a Free Agent can escape from company exploitation and from the salary adjustments that unions have traditionally enforced upon employees, preventing the meritorious from receiving higher salaries. Free Agents can optimize their income. Along with freedom comes the demand for 'marketability' – the ability to adapt to the services in demand. And along with freedom comes greater uncertainty about income, which may not necessarily be seen as a disadvantage; some IT people see it as a challenge to meet the needs of customers and to remain on the forefront of development.

The Field Story of 'Open-Source Grassrooter'

In *The Ha@ker Ethic*, Himanen (2001) tells how the Internet, World Wide Web (www), desktop computers and important software systems (for example Linux operating system) were created by and created 'hackers'[3] – and their way of organizing (see also Berners-Lee 2000; Levy 2001; Torvalds & Diamond 2001; http://mirror.opensource.dk; http://www.nessus.org; and http://www.tuxedo.org/~esr/writings/cathedral-bazar/). Himanen (2001) describes how the hacker ethics challenges society and the lives we live. Not all hackers comply with the ethical rules, but Himanen argues that the hackers must be seen as a whole. For a hacker, passion and hard work are two sides of the same coin, and Himanen quotes one as saying 'Being a hacker is lots of fun, but it's a kind of fun that takes a lot of effort'. A hacker is subscribing neither to a pre-Protestant ethic, in which Paradise was equivalent to life without work, or to Max Weber's Protestant Ethic, in which work is a duty. The new technology makes it easy to demolish the border between work and leisure time. But the implication in a hacker's version of time optimization is not that work absorbs all the available time. The hacker is not at the disposal of work twenty-four hours a day, but optimizes time in order to make room for play and other activities with no immediate direction.

In the new economy, the stress is not only on private ownership of capital, but also on information gathered via patents, copyrights and trade marks. In contrast, the hacker emphasizes openness and public ownership of information. Most important to the hacker is not money, but peer recognition of a good piece of code work. Not all hackers are reluctant to make money by hacking, but they do not want to gain financially from methods that require them to keep information from others. One of the key questions for the hacker is, therefore, whether it is possible to create a free market economy in which competition is not combined with control of information. Neither traditional capitalism nor communism provide answers to the problem. The hacker community does not know the answer, but the very raising of the question is viewed as a sufficient radical challenge.

The Field Story of the 'Project Maker in a Professional Community'

The fourth field story is about the IT project maker who is part of a team developing an exciting piece of IT software. The IT project maker is deeply committed to the development of the product, and loyal to the team that has been established for the purpose. But at the same time, project makers are part of several professional communities, through which they upgrade their technological knowledge.

In developing expertise, individuals are not concerned primarily with making themselves attractive in the market, but with developing and maintaining knowledge that is useful in the specific project. Therefore, we are currently witnessing the emergence of a series of new professional communities in which IT people meet and discuss concrete themes. But these communities are never related directly to the concrete projects in which they are individually involved. Certain of these communities are new organizations that emerge as associations of members or as private firms that offer professional IT people discussion arenas. Other communities emerge within, for example, unions, and contribute to their transformation from traditional organizations safeguarding member interests into professional development organizations (Buch 2002).

IT project makers who are dissatisfied with the environment for developing software – situations with incompetent, unprofessional colleagues or a management that restricts product development – will attempt to move to a different environment with better conditions. This is one of the reasons we are currently witnessing greater mobility in the labour market: IT people are moving towards the interesting projects.

Analysis of the Four Field Identity Stories

In all four stories, a subject – a 'me' – is evoked as an active and independent individual. This is, however, the only resemblance to identity construction, insofar as the 'mes' in the four stories have widely different connected relations to 'you' and instrumental relations to 'it'.

The first field story, about the Citizen in the Company, tells of an active and independent employee ('me') collaborating with other active and independent employees ('you'), and in concert they constitute a whole, in the form of the company ('us'). The individual is tied to the other employees in the company, and the company is here constructed as the homeland of the employees. At the same time, a distinction is made between the company and 'it' – that which lies outside and constitutes the market of the company and other relevant environments. 'It' contains, among other things and people, employees in other companies or people (for example freelancers and contractors) that migrate across company boundaries like nomads migrating across country borders. Such people are considered alien elements.

The second story, about the Free Agent in the Market, tells of an active and independent person ('me') selling his or her services. As such, the Free Agent is connected to others who are buying the services ('you'), and in combination they constitute the market. At the same time, a distinction is made in the story between the market and the hierarchical company ('it') as being oppressive and exploitative in relation to the Free Agent.

The third story, about the Open-Source Grassrooter, also evokes an active and independent individual. This person ('me') develops projects in collaboration with other active and independent individuals ('you') in an open community ('us'). Everybody is – via the Internet – in a position to join the open community, provided that they comply with certain codes for good behaviour. These are the codes that draw the frontier between what is evoked in the story as the open and closed communities ('it'); in the story companies usually represent the latter.

The fourth story, about the Project Maker in Professional Communities, tells of an active and independent professional – a 'me' – working with other professionals on concrete projects that constitute an 'us'. Furthermore, a different 'us' is evoked, one that is related to the professional communities in which norms for knowledge development are emerging, but which are void of concrete project work. On the other side of the border is 'it', which is characterized by non-professionalism.

The four field stories are not only recognizable as stories about IT workers, but have certain features in common with identity stories told in other spheres of work in contemporary society. I do not pursue this point here.

Thus furnished with four identity stories that are widely distributed in the IT field, I now proceed to analyse what takes place in practice. Here I demonstrate how the four stories are put into play and transformed through negotiations among the actors involved in work practice.

Table 6.1 Dimensions in four field identity stories

Dimensions in the analysis of identities Four Field Identity Stories	'ME'	'YOU'	'US'	'IT'
CITIZEN IN THE COMPANY	Active and independent IT employee	Other employees and managers in the company	The company	The market
FREE AGENT IN THE MARKET	Active and independent provider of IT services	Purchasers of IT services	The market	Bureaucratic and exploiting companies
OPEN-SOURCE GRASSROOTER	Active and independent IT developer	Other IT developers	The open community	Closed companies
PROJECT MAKER IN PROFESSIONAL COMMUNITIES	Active and independent IT professional	The other IT professionals	Project team and professional communities	The non-professionals

131

PRACTICE IDENTITIES STORIES (EMERGING NEGOTIATED IDENTITIES) – THREE EXAMPLES

John in Practice

In the field story about the open-source community, there is a tendency to distinguish between work and leisure time, and grassroots participation in the open community is often described as a leisure activity – it is something one does at home and outside working hours. This is where the fun and wild IT activities are conducted, as opposed to the set IT tasks for which employees and consultants are paid. On my voyage in the IT field, I encountered – contrary to the above-mentioned assumption – temporary employees in companies that drew on open sources in their daily work. I also encountered companies whose business recipe and work practice were built upon the open source idea, in that it combined the commercial economic world and the world of open knowledge. The following section describes the negotiated identities related to the owner (John) of one of these firms.

John was about forty years old, and worked in the media world in the past. In the mid-1990s, he started an IT firm. In 2000, he wanted to publish a product he had developed as an open-source programme, in order to disseminate it and encourage others to elaborate on it. The concept of open source was a new phenomenon defined in 1998. John had learned about it from a programmer with whom he had collaborated. He was attracted by the idea because, as he says:

> It makes knowledge sharing possible. I think that what we are doing is universal, and should be accessible for all applications involving our product. Therefore it made sense to involve people working with similar problems in the development of the basic functions. Based on these functions, tailor-made solutions could be developed for various customers.

During 2000, John became increasingly burdened with debts that required him to find venture capital. Although he succeeded in attracting capital, the venture capitalists would not accept open source as part of their business recipe. John was sacked, and in early 2001, found himself without a firm.

John mortgaged his flat and hired three employees, who have developed a new model from scratch. As their point of departure, they downloaded an open programme from the Internet, further developed it, and subsequently uploaded the elaborated version, making it available for others. In further developing the programme, they collaborated with IT programmers who formally worked in other places, while simultaneously working openly on the Internet. As John says:

To resolve problems at the same speed as was possible via the Internet would require several hundred employees. Many of the problems concern very specific issues, and when we inquire on the Internet it is rarely more than 24 hours before we have one or several responses.

But even as John's employees draw their knowledge from the Internet, others have started to ask them questions via the Internet. If the questions concern issues that do not interest them but are easily resolved, they respond. As one of John's employees says, 'It's cool being able to produce something that others can use and to help some of the guys in the USA that you admire: just do so and so'. Being able to respond to questions gives people status in the open-source community. But as John says: 'We don't spend a week correcting errors for somebody in the USA if it isn't something that we can use'.

John's firm makes money by adapting the product to the specific needs of specific customers. If Microsoft had developed the product, similar adaptations to customer needs would be required. The difference is that had Microsoft developed the product, the customer would have to pay a start fee, which is not the case when the product is available as an open-source programme. The advantage for John's firm is, however, that having developed the product, it occupies the cutting edge. It will take some time before others become equally adept at adapting it to customer-specific needs. But it also means that the firm must compete for producing the best quality rather than dominating the market and leaving customers with few other options.

John says that his firm rests on

> a reverse line of thought in relation to traditional economy and business strategy. It has taken a long time and we have been subject to great ridicule, but it has been fun to see that the customers now realise the great advantage of our approach. They have started to demand open-source products. The concept suddenly starts to spread – and quickly now.

Sometimes the firm is also involved in the development of closed-systems products, as when the firm collaborates with hardware producers who are working with closed codes. But the closure is immaterial, according to John, because the product cannot be used in other contexts. 'It's fine. There are situations in which it is better to produce your own things and keep them as business secrets, particularly if it concerns a very specific area.' Nevertheless he admits that other programmers may be able to transfer the codes to other situations, but the company with which John collaborates will not concede openness for the product. He has accepted this condition, because 'It's worth more to us to produce this for XXX under the conditions which they stipulate. Then we can work for others in the way we prefer. So in the case of XXX, we work with a closed system.' John estimates that about 10 per cent of the firm's jobs involve working with closed codes, and he does not expect this share to change to any appreciable extent.

Tom in Practice

The second example derives from a medium-sized Danish IT company, Teccom, located south of Copenhagen. I visited this firm and its development department of 35 IT developers for a couple of days in 2000 and 2001. The developers work in-house at Teccom, and are developing the company's own software products. Although 75 per cent of the IT workers are permanently employed, 25 per cent – the so-called 'consultants' – are contracted for three to six months. According to the manager, the firm hires temporary consultants because it has experienced high rates of personnel turnover.

Observing the IT developers, it was impossible to distinguish the permanent employees from the temporary consultants, and one of the latter was once taken for a permanent employee by a newly-appointed IT developer. But delineation exists. The company distinguishes between permanent employees and consultants through language: temporaries are referred to as 'consultants'. The two groups are also distinguished at the organizational level, for consultants are not allowed to participate in the morning meetings where the managers inform the permanent employees about developments in Teccom, and where common problems are discussed. At the material level, consultants are not equipped with laptops like the permanent employees are, and the consultants are provided with desktop computers of a quality inferior to that of the permanent employees. Furthermore, consultants cannot log on to the intranet from home, do not have access to all databases, and are not invited to such social events as the Christmas lunch. Even though the permanent employees and the consultants use a friendly and sociable tone among themselves, an informal boundary exists, reflected in such comments by the permanent employees as 'you – the expensive consultants'. When the permanent employees leave for lunch in the Teccom canteen, which is located in a different building, the consultants stay behind, and I have yet to see any of the consultants taking a break by playing darts like the permanent employees do after lunch.

The company views the consultants as labour hired to solve specific tasks, and the expectation is that the consultant is used to chaos and will perform quickly. The company experiences a significant problem in ensuring that consultants are given the time to document what they have been doing before 'signing off', as the project leader expresses it.

One of the consultants – Tom – works as a freelancer and has contacts with another IT company ZZZ that finds jobs for him. This company has – through two additional company contacts – connected him with Teccom. All the links in the chain make a profit on the next one – how much he does not know for sure – but his agreement with Teccom requires that he get 80 per cent and that Company ZZZ get 20 per cent He is paid €64 an hour, and guesses that Teccom ends up paying about €133 an hour for his services (an accurate guess, as it transpires). He estimates that he is paid, on average, twice as much as the permanent employees. Had the links between him and Teccom been fewer, his salary would have been higher. However, he does not negotiate directly with the companies that hire him, because he has few contacts. Tom has been with Teccom for five months and the contract is expiring in a couple of months. In his opinion, Teccom does not distinguish seriously between permanent employees and consultants, apart from morning meetings and the Christmas lunch. He finds it frustrating not to be part of the morning meetings, because they would yield information that he must subsequently try to obtain in different ways. But at the same time there are things, he says, 'that are of no concern to us' (by 'us', he means the consultants). Yet he has not been included in such meetings in his previous consulting jobs. He had worked earlier as a permanently employed consultant, but has opted out of this career in favour of the life of a freelancer. His experience as a permanently employed consultant tells him that there are too many managers involved. He thinks that by working as a freelancer he is in a better position to choose interesting jobs, such as his current work at Teccom.

The fact that he is an 'external' makes him cautious about the possible harmful effects of speaking negatively about his colleagues. On the other hand, he can talk confidentially with the people in Company ZZZ that find jobs for him. He feels more closely related to the other consultants he is collaborating with in Teccom than to the permanent employees.

> You can talk about other things [with the consultants]. About jobs in other companies – and about management [in Teccom], which is just too poor. You are bound to air a more positive attitude when talking with the permanent employees. They may be hurt personally in some way ... Nevertheless some of your opinions you can convey [to the permanently employed project leader] in a nice way, such as, 'It seems to be the official policy of Teccom to use development tools that are free'. And if I talk with the other consultants about it, I would say, 'It is dammed useless giving a craftsman whom you pay €133 an hour an old rotten spade and then asked him to make you a piece of furniture.' They're wasting their money, but you cannot put it that way to the project leader.

Teccom is not the only company in which Tom has experienced consultants being given poorer tools and working conditions, but it is worse in Teccom; it emphasizes the fact that consultants are not on a par with the others. So the life of a freelancer can be tough, which is naturally a disadvantage. But the advantage is that you can escape ennui and poor management. Tom says:

I usually get bored with a place after a year. Too little is happening. And I often disagree with the management. I find that they lack ambition. In a way they are not keeping themselves updated. Many of them are thinking about the survival of the company, but there is too much focus on the bottom line rather then on 'What are we actually doing here?'

In the long run, it is not Tom's plan to continue working as a consultant. He wants to work in a place where he can engage in long-term projects and where he is a proper member of a team. But that takes good management, so he concludes by saying that he would prefer to be permanently employed in his own company.

Anna in Practice

The third example derives from a new IT company, IT-SYS, in the northern part of Copenhagen that I visited in 2000 and revisited in 2001. The company had about forty employees, some of whom worked in-house developing the company's own products or solving customer problems; others worked in client companies producing tailored IT solutions. The outside workers, representing 25 per cent of the employees, were never referred to as consultants, but as 'body shoppers'. Those working in-house were located in two large rooms. People would pass through continually, talking informally about ongoing jobs and cracking jokes. One day a woman came into the room in which I was temporarily located. She greeted everyone in English, and they returned her greeting warmly. There were a couple of witty remarks about people she had met abroad who knew some of the people present. She had just returned from Helsinki, Finland, where she had been working for the first four days of the week – a work rhythm she had become accustomed to over the last couple of months. Her name was Anna and she was one of the body shoppers.

Anna is a Polish engineer in her late twenties who came to Denmark a couple of years ago when she married a Dane. She has been working with IT-SYS as a programmer since the company started. She is working temporarily as an expatriate in Finland, solving a special task for a client. The job arose when the Finnish company for which Anna is undertaking the task approached a Finnish IT company that in turn approached a Danish partner, Company YYY. The latter turned to a Danish agency, asking it to find IT workers. The agency approached IT-SYS, inquiring if it had employees capable of performing the task, and Anna had the competencies. When she is in Finland she works with people employed by the Danish IT Company YYY, and with programmers in the Finnish client company.

In the beginning, Anna worked with another IT-SYS employee in Finland, and between the two of them they had to figure out the nature of the situation. Nobody told them who they would be working with, the status of the product, or what type of documentation was available. They spent the first three weeks figuring out the status of the job.

After having travelled between Denmark and Finland for three months, Anna says:

> I stay up there four days a week. So I come back for the weekend. It is difficult. I love the project. I love my colleagues, both at IT-SYS and YYY, and I like the system how we work; it's very interesting. It is a way to learn, and learning is allowed, and I enjoy that they can use me. It is a very nice experience. But in the same time, I don't have any private life. My husband is sitting here and waiting for me. He works a lot as well. He misses me. So, I just eat and work to midnight or one or two o'clock, and then I start again next morning. It is very hard. But it is nice.

IT-SYS has decided that Anna is to spend one day a week in the company because, as Anna says:

> They said that I need to have a life connection to my mother company. I want to be back, see them and talk with them, and do whatever I can. Usually I am doing some small parts of some projects. Small tasks I can do on Fridays. It is very nice to be back and talk with people, and I am very happy ... It is easy – very easy [to come back to IT-SYS]. But it really was difficult when we started to employ new people. Then it was something else, because I would introduce myself, but they forgot me after a week. I can't have the same connection to them as I have to my [old] IT-SYS colleagues.

If Anna needs help in solving some of the problems she encounters as a programmer, she turns to her colleagues at IT-SYS and Company YYY, and to the public places on the Internet where others have uploaded solutions that she can download for free. She says that it is

> somehow like a community. They have this attitude: 'I have found this solution to that problem' ... It is a community in which everybody can learn. In my view these people are nerds. Programming is their life. This means that they spend their leisure time on programming as well. And they are incredibly happy if they get feedback from others. And sometimes the responses are suggestions for different ways of solving the problem ... So there are many different types of feedback from which you can learn.'

Anna has not yet uploaded anything on the Internet – for two reasons. First, she wants to make sure that what she uploads is correct. Second, 'I am not the nerd type. I don't want to spend all my time on IT. I don't spend time on solving small jobs on the Internet. But now we're talking about it, there might be something that I can upload'.

When I visited IT-SYS half a year later, Anna had just returned from her job in Finland. The original plan was that she should spend a maximum of two months in Finland, but it turned into more than six months. Half way through the period, the project team had been replaced, and during the six months she had been working with six or seven new employees from the Danish IT company, YYY. Furthermore, an international consultancy and a number of employees in the Finnish company had been attached to the job.

Anna had told me previously that when in Finland she was not supposed to say that she is employed in IT-SYS and she hated lying about her true company affiliation. Six months later, it is still only her closest colleagues employed in YYY who know she is not working for YYY. But it no longer poses a problem to her 'because as soon as I sign a contract with the IT company, YYY, and as soon as I am introduced to the project, then I am introduced to their work methods and I offer my services as a YYY employee – and there is nothing wrong with that'.

Anna continued returning to IT-SYS in Denmark one day a week if the work pressure in the Finnish company allowed for it. But things changed. She was unable to get involved in one-day projects in IT-SYS, and old colleagues left and new ones arrived. So in the end she was administering her YYY work, while spending a day in IT-SYS.

YYY had offered her a job, and after thinking it over for a long time, she accepted; there were a number of university-educated IT people at YYY who knew much more than she did and from whom she could learn. But being employed by YYY was not without its problems, in that IT-SYS had signed a contract with an IT agency at the time when they body-shopped Anna to YYY. According to that contract, Anna could not accept a job with YYY without YYY paying a considerable amount of money to the agency. So Anna is prevented from working with YYY for a year. Her last remark is that she is in the process of growing and finding out what she wants in the future. In the long-term she does not want to combine children and family with sitting glued to the screen doing programming jobs.

Analysis of Three Examples from Practice

In Figure 6.1, I have systematized the emergence of identities in work practices. I argue that widely distributed field identity stories exists about what it means to work with IT. In the concrete IT work practice, arenas of meaning are currently developed in which the actors ascribe meaning to concrete events by drawing on field identity stories and negotiating concrete identities.

John: emerging from 'Open-Source Grassrooter' to becoming an 'Open-Source Grassrooter on universal themes and Citizen in the Company on very specific themes'
The story about John begins with his relating to the open-source community that has developed throughout the 1990s in the IT field. In this relationship he

Emerging identities beyond organizational boundaries

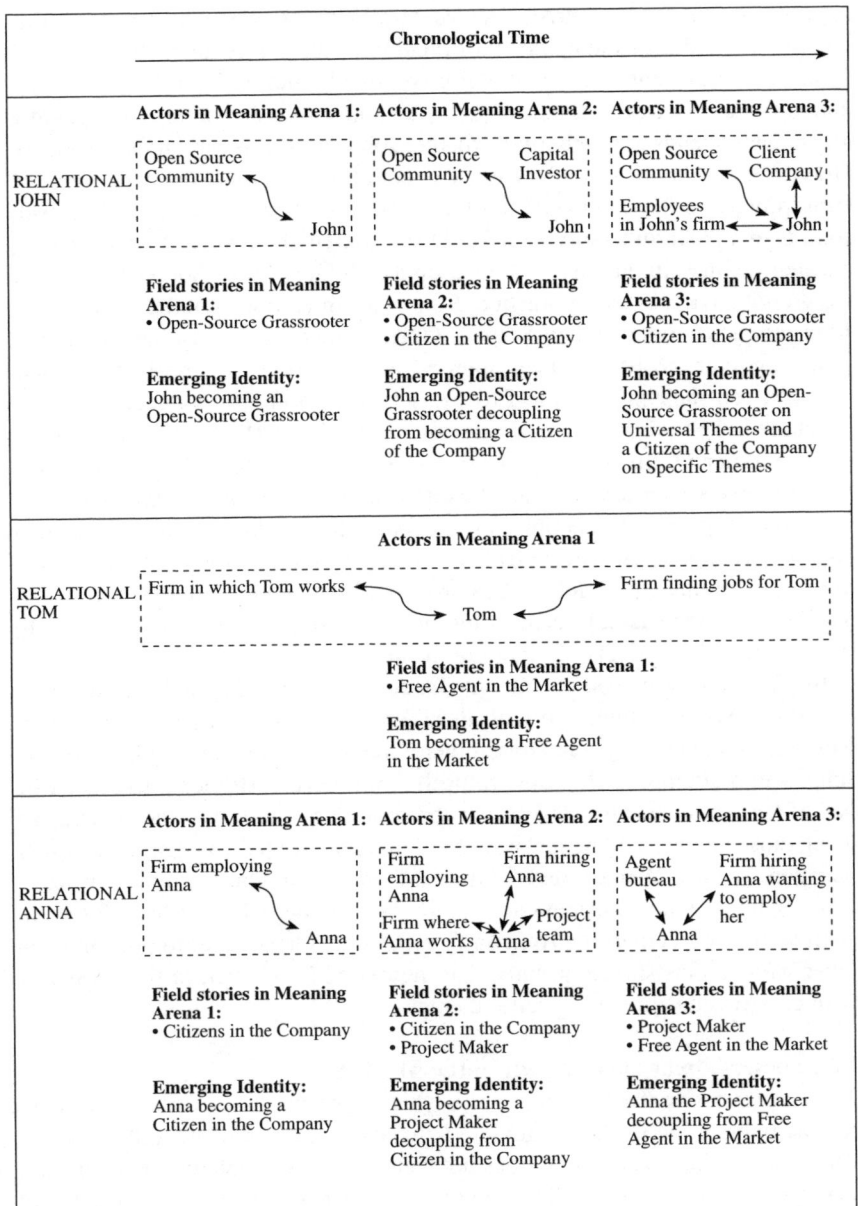

Figure 6.1 Three emerging identities in work practice

appears as an Open-Source Grassrooter. Without the emergence of this community and his establishment of relations with it, it is difficult to see how John could have entered business life so quickly and with so little friction – and survived. Because of John's debt, a capital investor enters the meaning arena, which leads to a fight over whether John can survive as an Open-Source Grassrooter. The fight ends with a decoupling of John, the Open-Source Grassrooter, on the one hand, and the capital investor on the other. In effect, John is in a position to survive as an Open-Source Grassrooter by mortgaging his apartment. Without this or another option, John as Open-Source Grassrooter would not have worked in practice. Being part of an open-source community, John employs other Open-Source Grassrooters, and they are mutually affirming their identity as Open-Source Grassrooters. This is possible because they can sell their products to firms in which they apply products they have developed. The products are accessible on the Internet; that is, they can be used by other IT firms for application in client companies. But the fact that John and his employees have developed the products means that they are a few steps ahead of their competitors in the application of the products. With this competitive advantage, their identity – as Open-Source Grassrooters – works in practice. Being Open-Source Grassrooters, John and his employees prosper, as clients are increasingly demanding open-source products as alternatives to the closed-code products of other companies.

But John has also been in contact with customers that demand closed codes. If John wants to collaborate with these customers, he must step back from working as an Open-Source Grassrooter. One would immediately assume that John would attempt to decouple himself from these customers, given that he has other customers. But this is not the case. He enters into the practice of using closed codes, and he make sense of this practice by establishing a border between 'specific themes' and 'universal themes'. In relation to the former, it is acceptable to have business secrets. During the period that I have followed John he has been emerging from an Open-Source Grassrooter to becoming an Open-Source Grassrooter in universal themes and a Citizen in the Company with closed codes in very specific themes.

Tom: emerging as 'Free Agent in the Market'
The employees in the IT company in which Tom works evoke a story about him as being alien to them: they are Citizens in the Company and he is not. But being defined as an alien does not cause identity problems for Tom, as it matches his own understanding of himself as a freelancer. Being a Free Agent in the Market, he has no desire to become a Citizen in the Company in which he works. Neither does he have identity problems in relation to the IT company that finds him jobs. They negotiate contracts, selling him to other companies, which is fully in keeping with his perception of himself as a Free

Agent.[4] Tom appears as a stranger in the company in which he works, but he also appears as a Free Agent and there is no contradiction between the two. Therefore there are no negotiations in the meaning arena, but a reproduction of Tom's identity as a Free Agent and a stranger in the company.

Anna emerging from 'Citizen in the Company' to becoming 'Project Maker in Professional Communities'

Prior to working as an expatriate in Finland, Anna worked physically in IT-SYS, where she is currently employed. Here Anna is engaged in relationships in which only one identity story is evoked through speech – that of Anna and the other employees in IT-SYS as Citizens in the Company – and she herself is also telling this story about herself and her colleagues in IT-SYS.

As long as Anna works in IT-SYS, her identity as Citizen in the Company works well within her relationships. But when the company sends her to Finland, that is no longer the case. Even though IT-SYS wants her to stick to the citizen identity, it no longer makes sense to her unequivocally, as she is no longer part of the IT-SYS community's common tasks and social life. Nevertheless, she seems to do fine in Finland without a clear IT-SYS citizenship – and the Danish Company YYY which hired her for the job actually demands that she does not refer to herself as an IT-SYS employee. On the other hand, she finds it problematic having to pretend to be a member of the YYY staff. She does not resolve this pressure by changing her IT-SYS citizenship for a YYY citizenship, but by shifting the focus from her employment with IT-SYS to her concrete project in Finland, where she applies YYY software. She thus emerges from a Citizen in the Company to becoming a Project Maker, and this shift is further supported by some of the other relationships in which Anna is engaged – especially her relationship with other IT people with whom she is working closely in Finland.

Towards the end of the period in which I followed her, yet another actor enters the meaning arena – the agency that has mediated Anna's temporary transfer from IT-SYS to Company YYY. The reason is that YYY wants to employ Anna, who is interested in a position with YYY, as the company can offer attractive project work. But the agency is unwilling to concede to the transfer, which it is contractually able to prevent. The alternative is a large penalty that YYY must pay the agency for having 'stolen its commodity'. The agency's business concept is to mediate the sale and purchase of IT people (in this case, Anna) to companies and between companies and freelancers, and it will not accept that its commodities (IT people) vanish from the market, which would be the case if Anna independently accepted employment with YYY. Anna did not know anything about the contents of the contract. Had she perceived of herself as a Free Agent – which she does not – this would not have come as a surprise to her. In any case, she rejects the idea of seeing herself as a commodity. To her, the story of the Free Agent becomes a story that leaves regulatory trails (for example prevents her from working with existing projects). But it does not become a story in which she is described in terms of identity. Regulatively, she cannot decouple herself from the story though.

CONCLUSION

In the chapter I analyse emerging identities in temporary and scattered work practices. The analysis conceals diverse agendas.

First, I argue that identities are not static phenomena that are permanently bonded to individuals, but dynamic phenomena that emerge in practice. A person's identity (subject position) is evoked through speech in stories that give meaning in practice (they work in practice). The meaning is constructed in relation to the boundaries among the person's 'me', 'you', 'us', and 'it' – what is evoked in the stories. In the analysis, I identify four relevant identity stories: the Citizen in the Company, the Free Agent in the Market, the Open-Source Grassrooter, and the Project Maker in the Professional Community. I argue that identities are socially constructed, whether the identity remains the same or changes. That is, the boundaries evoked through speech in relation to 'me', 'you', 'us', and 'it' are either reproduced or displaced. This is illustrated in the analysis with a description of how three persons develop subject positions from different stories (combining Open-Source Grassrooter and Citizen in the Company); reproduce subject positions (the Free Agent in the Market), or exchange the subject position of one story for that of another one (from Citizen in the Company to Project Maker in Professional Communities).

In the introduction I challenged Sennett's assumption on the corrosion of character in the flexible economy. My empirical analysis seems to support the criticism: the analysis shows that even though individuals in temporary and scattered work practices are in situations in which their well-known identities are subject to pressure, the implication is not unilateral loss of identity, but rather the emergency of identity. The temporary and scattered work practice that I have described involves significant efforts in creating identity.

Second, I argue that identities are not individual phenomena. Quite the contrary, they are network phenomena or relational phenomena. In this context, two points are important. First, my analytical point of departure is that a person's 'me' is tied to certain specific surroundings – 'you', 'us', and 'it'. In effect, a description of a person's identity is not only a description of 'me', as the 'me' is indescribable without relational demarcation. Both sides of this demarcation are enacted simultaneously. It is the relationship between 'me' and diverse surroundings that delineates a person's identity. As a consequence of this argument, it is not possible to talk about, for example, a Free Agent without understanding that a Free Agent can only exist in a market, and that the Free Agent in the Market is alien to the Citizen in the Company. Second, an identity is subject to stabilization or change in processes in which relationships among actors determine whether or not an identity works. To capture these processes, I propose an analytical tool that I call a meaning arena; it not only focuses on the actors, but also on the relationships among actors in the meaning arena.

Third, I focus on work practice as the key pivot for identity development, as opposed to, for example, studies of employment relations that seem to be the central pivot in many human resource management (HRM) and industrial relations (IR) studies. The researchers in HRM and IR studies often seem to assume that individual identities are dependent upon, in particular, whether individuals are employed long-term (which is often considered typical) or employed on short-term contracts, part-time employment, on a freelance basis or independently (discussed under the common denominator: atypical employment). Such employment conditions may play a role in the social construction of identities, but I do not wish to begin with such presumptions. Rather, I have directed my focus toward the concept of work practice as the central location for the social construction. In other words, where HRM and IR studies discuss employment relations as a variable – often an exogenous variable – I view work practice as a melting pot for meaning creation.

Fourth, I argue that analysing temporary and scattered work practice is interesting in that it questions the organization theory assumption of the appropriateness of operating within the boundaries of an organization. Within organization theory, this boundary is often of decisive analytical import, when the analysis concerns such factors as the strategies and the management of organizations. I argue that 'organizational boundaries' are socially constructed empirical phenomena, and it is quite probable that employees in temporary and scattered work practices evoke through speech, boundaries that differ from those conceptualized by employees working permanently together in the same location (see for example Westenholz 2003). These different constructions of the company and its boundaries will – I assume – have far-reaching consequences for management activities in companies. They mean, among other things, that managers must be understood as actors in relation (network) to other actors in the meaning arena. These arenas develop in relation to practical problems emerging in temporary and scattered work practices. Managers are not in control of the identity stories negotiated in the meaning arena, but they can be part of the negotiations by attempting to evoke, through speech, specific identity stories – often about the Citizen in the Company. Whether this is a sensible strategy compared to innovation within IT is a different story.

Finally, I have tried in this analysis to give priority to neither the macro nor the micro level. I have attempted to evoke an analysis in which I focus on the ways in which widely distributed stories in an organizational IT field (field identity stories) gain ground and are transformed in work practices (practice identity stories). Some people will be inclined to refer to field identity stories as macro phenomena and to practice identity stories as micro phenomena. But as it appears from my analysis, both field and practice stories are interwoven, and the micro-macro distinction is not consistent with the data.

NOTES

1. Data were derived from the research project *Relational Identities in Temporary and Scattered Work Practice*, conducted at the Copenhagen Business School, 2000–04, by Torben Elgaard Jensen, David Metz and Ann Westenholz.
2. In line with DiMaggio and Powell (1991, pp. 64–5), I understand the IT field as consisting of actors (organizations and individuals) that constitute a distinguishable institutional IT work field: key suppliers, resources, product consumers, regulatory agencies, unions, professional associations, grassroots movements, agencies and other organizations producing IT products. As DiMaggio and Powell stress, this field concept points towards the totality of relevant actors that must be defined through empirical studies. The IT field is relatively novel and there is continuous change in its patterns of interaction and dominance, the quantity of information that actors in the field must take into consideration, and the common attention among the actors who are involved in IT work. Several diverse understandings of the IT field may be at play simultaneously. In this chapter I do not specify the IT field in detail, but apply it as a concept suitable for delimiting a wide range of IT work within which recognizable stories are told about identities in the field.
3. Himanen applies the 'hacker' concept in a specific way, in that he distinguishes between hackers and crackers. The latter is a person who breaks into and spreads viruses in information systems. As it appears from Himanen's anecdote, a hacker is quite a different person – a hero rather than a criminal. In common parlance, however, the word 'hacker' is used to denote a person who spreads viruses. Therefore in order to avoid misunderstandings I have chosen to name the story about these people the story about 'open-source grassrooters'. But because I use Himanen's text, I also use the Himanerian conception of 'hacker'.
4. Tom's identity as a Free Agent in the Market does not make him more independent than John and Anna of the relationships from which his identity emerges; all of their identities emerge within relationships.

REFERENCES

Aley, J. (1995), 'The Temp Biz Book: Why it's Good', *Fortune*, **16**, 53–5.
Berners-Lee, T. (2000), *Weaving the Web: The Original Design and Ultimate Destiny of the World Wide Web by its Inventor*, New York: Harper-Collins.
Bridges, W. (1994), *Job Shift: How to Prosper in a Workplace Without Jobs*, Reading, Mass.: Perseus Books.
Buch, A. (2002), *The Society of Danish Engeneers – More Than a Union*, Paper presented at 18th EGOS Colloquium, Barcelona, Sub-theme 15: Temporary and Scattered Work Practice.
Budtz, C. and C. Moseholm (2000), 'Farvel til Corporate Religion', *Ledelse i dag*, **10** (5), 443–5.

Christensen, S. and A. Westenholz (1999), *Medarbejdervalgte i Danske Virksomheder: Fra Lønarbejder til Borger i Virksomhedssamfundet*, Copenhagen: Handelshøjskolens Forlag.
Davies, B. and R. Harré (1990), 'Positioning: The Discursive Production of Selves', *Journal of the Theory Social Behaviour*, **2**, 43–64.
DiMaggio, P.J. and W.W. Powell (1991), 'The Iron Cage Revisited: Institutional Isomorphism and Collective Rationality', in W.W. Powell and P.J. DiMaggio (eds), *The New Institutionalism in Organizational Analysis*, Chicago: The University of Chicago Press.
Emirbayer, M. (1997), 'Manifesto for a Relational Sociology', *American Journal of Sociology*, **103** (2), 281–317.
Ezzy, D. (1998), 'Theorizing Narative Identity: Symbolic Interactionism and Hermeneutics', *The Sociological Quarterly*, **39** (2), 239–52.
Flecker, J. and J. Hofbauer (1998), 'Capitalising on Subjectivity: The "New Model Worker" and the Importance of Being Useful', in P. Thompson and C. Warhurst (eds), *Workplaces of the Future*, London: Macmillan Business.
Gergen, K.J. (1994), *Realities and Relationships: Soundings in Social Construction*, Cambridge, Mass.: Harvard University Press.
Gergen, K.J. (1999), *An Invitation to Social Construction*, London: Sage Publications.
Gergen, K.J. (2001), *Social Construction in Context*, London: Sage Publications.
Hall, S. (1996), 'Introduction: Who Needs "Identity?"', in S. Hall and P. Du Gay (eds), *Questions of Cultural Identity*, London: Sage Publications.
Himanen, P. (2001), *The Ha@ker Ethic: A Radical Approach to the Philosophy of Business*, New York: Random House Trade Paperbacks.
Levy, S. (2001), *Hackers: Heroes of the Computer Revolution*, New York: Delta.
Mandag Morgen (1999), '25 Millioner "Free Agents" Omformer Amerikansk Politik', *Mandag Morgen*, **31**, 16–19.
Miller, P. and N. Rose (1995), 'Production, Identity, and Democracy', *Theory and Society*, **24**, 427–67.
Pink, D.H. (2001), *Free Agent Nation*, New York: Warner Books, Inc.
Sennett, R. (1998), *The Corrosion of Character: The Personal Consequences of Work in the New Capitalism*, New York: W.W. Norton & Company.
Stokholm, Frank (2001), 'Eliten Letter', *Børsens Nyhedsmagasin*, **6**, February, 19–25, 38–42.
Torvalds, L. and D. Diamond (2001), *Just for Fun: The Story of an Accidental Revolutionary*, New York: Texere.
Weick, K. (1995), *Sensemaking in Organizations*, Thousand Oaks: Sage Publications.
Westenholz, A. (2003), 'Organizational Citizen: Unionized Wage Earners, Participate Management and Beyond', in B. Czarniawska and G. Sevón (eds), *The Northern Lights: Organization Theory in Scandinavia*, Copenhagen: Copenhagen Business School.

ACKNOWLEDGEMENTS

I am very grateful to Citizens in the Companies, Project Makers in Professional Communities, Free Agents and Open-Source Grassrooters (and all sorts of combinations of the four) within the IT field, who shared their insights and stories with me. I also want to thank colleagues who commented on earlier versions of this chapter: Torben Elgaard Jensen, David Metz and participants from the book seminar at Klitgaarden, Skagen, August 2003. Marianne Risberg and Nina Colwill have been very helpful in preparing the typescript in English.

Afterword: the tyranny of the epochal and work identity

Paul du Gay

THE EPOCHAL

As the contributions to this volume indicate, one of the most striking things about much contemporary theorizing about work and identity – whether critical or managerial in orientation – is the epochalist terms in which it is framed. By the term 'epochalist', we are referring to the use of a periodizing schema in which a logic of dichotomization establishes the available terms of debate in advance, either for or against. As Tom Osborne (1998, p. 17) has indicated with reference to contemporary social theories, epochal accounts

> are those which seek to encapsulate the Zeitgeist in some kind of overarching societal designation; that we live in a postmodern society, a modern society, an information society, a rationalised society, a risk society ... Such epochal ... theories tend to set up their co-ordinates in advance, leaving no 'way out' from their terms of reference.

Whether the theorizing in question is being conducted by Zygmunt Bauman (2000 – 'Liquid Modernity'), Scott Lash and John Urry (1994 – 'Economies of Signs'), Manuel Castells (2000 – 'The Network Society'), Tom Peters (1992 – 'Chaos' or 'Crazy Times') or Charles Leadbeater (1999 – 'The Knowledge Driven Economy'), and whether the interpretation proffered is bitterly pessimistic or dizzyingly optimistic, the common denominator is an epochalist emphasis. Indeed, such is the standing of epochal analysis, not only within the social and management sciences, but also within the worlds of public policy and business strategy, that discussion of a given issue – 'globalization', 'work', 'identity' and so on – becomes almost invariably framed in 'epochal' terms. A couple of pertinent examples should suffice.

In recent years, certain arguments have been advanced in the social sciences – often associated with terms such as 'economies of signs', 'the network society' and 'the knowledge economy' – that we are living in an era in which economic and organizational life and work identity has become thoroughly 'culturalized' (see McFall, this volume for a detailed treatment of this theme).

One of the most sustained attempts to make this argument is contained in Lash and Urry's *Economies of Signs and Space*. Here, it is argued that

> Economic and symbolic processes are more than ever interlaced and interarticulated; that is ... the economy is increasingly culturally inflected and ... culture is more and more economically inflected. Thus, the boundaries between the two become more and more blurred and the economy and culture no longer function in regard to one another as system and environment (1994, p. 64).

In attempting to back up this claim that the economy is now more than ever 'culturalized', Lash and Urry point to a number of developments. For instance, they claim that organizations whose business involves the production and distribution of cultural hardware and software have become the most innovative and entrepreneurial economic actors in the world today. The 'creative' or 'culture' industries broadly defined and other 'soft' knowledge-intensive industries not only represent the most important economic growth sectors, but also offer paradigmatic instances of the generalized process of 'de-differentiation' of economy/culture relations (1994, p. 108–9).

At the same time, Lash and Urry argue that a fundamental shift has taken place in the extent to which meaning is attached to products and services. They argue that more and more of the goods and services produced for consumers across a range of sectors can be conceived of as 'cultural goods', in that they are deliberately and instrumentally inscribed with particular meanings and associations as they are produced and circulated in a conscious attempt to generate desire for them among end users. As such, 'what is increasingly produced is not material objects but signs' (1994, p. 4). They assert that there is a growing aestheticization or fashioning of, often seemingly banal, products where these are marketed to consumers in terms of particular clusters of meaning, often linked to 'lifestyles', and this is taken as an indication of the radically increased importance of 'culture' to the production and circulation of a multitude of goods and services. This process, they argue, has been accompanied by the increased influence of what are often termed the 'cultural intermediary' occupations of advertising, design and marketing (See the chapter by Van Wijk and Leisink, this volume).

Lash and Urry's account of contemporary economic and organizational change can be described as epochalist in that it is both founded upon and sustains a dualism that is also a periodization. A dualism is posited between 'use value' and 'sign value', for instance, which is then used to frame two loosely periodized epochs – the less culturally inflected past (Fordism, as they have it) and the thoroughly culturalized present (Aesthetically Reflexive Post-Fordism/Postmodernism). In so doing, they reduce a range of economic, social and organizational changes to one or two 'overarching' and fundamental characteristics. Clearly, reductionism is necessary to any periodization –

otherwise we are in danger of reproducing the 'one damn thing after another' approach to historical explanation. However, it is important to note that the empirical significance of these epochal claims does need careful consideration. After all, authors working in fields as diverse as organization studies, the social anthropology of economic life and the history of advertising, for example, have indicated just how empirically unsubstantiated are the exemplary oppositions – between a more 'use-value' centred past and a more 'sign-value' centred present – that run through epochalist accounts such as this (Douglas and Isherwood 1979; McFall, this volume). Perhaps much of the hyperbole surrounding epochal claims of 'increased culturalization' can be explained by the fact that those taking the 'cultural turn' in the field of economic and organizational analysis are busy finding culture where none was thought to exist. However, they also tend, perhaps, to work against the grain of 'cultural economic' analysis, as an emergent form of inquiry concerned with the practical material-cultural ways in which 'economic' and 'organizational' objects and identities are put together, by, as Osborne (1998, p. 19) has it, setting up their co-ordinates too far in advance and thus leaving 'no way out' from their terms of reference. This has the effect of rendering certain potentially significant, if (seen from the heights of the epochal mindset) often seemingly banal, contextual details unimportant or invisible. After all, techniques of economic and organizational management rarely come ready-made. They have to be invented, implanted, stabilized and reproduced. This involves much hard, frequently tedious work, whose success and effects cannot be taken for granted 'in advance'. Thus the emergence of such techniques are probably not best explicated in terms of large-scale transformative processes – transitions from Fordism to Post-Fordism or from the 'old' to the 'new' economy, and so on – beloved of epochal theorizing, but rather cry out for the 'grey, meticulous and patiently documentary' forms of analysis recommended by (the rather more straight-laced and thus perhaps somewhat underappreciated) Foucault (1986, p. 76) among many others (Callon 1998; Law 1994, 2002). This should not be taken to imply an out-and-out rejection of all claims of 'increased culturalization'. Clearly, there are any number of substantive developments in organizational life – such as the recent obsession with managing 'culture' among senior executives of many enterprises – that might conceivably be explicable in terms of some suitably situated 'culturalization' hypothesis. However, it is important that such claims be assessed with care and on more of a case-by-case basis – as the contributors to the present volume have shown – rather than simply being assumed or asserted. As Paul DiMaggio (1994, p. 27) has argued, for example, in relation to the upsurge of interest in all things 'cultural' in the field of economic and organizational analysis, 'the price of the insights and explanatory power that a cultural perspective can generate is an enduring scepticism towards "culturalist" accounts that claim too much or generalise too broadly'.

If Lash and Urry's account is epochalist – tending towards an over-dramatic dichotomization which not only renders important contextual details insignificant if not entirely invisible, but also makes the changes they outline appear largely inevitable and hence incontrovertible – then the work of Tom Peters (1987, 1992, 1994) is the same, but much more so.

Clearly, Peters is not involved in the same practice as Lash and Urry. His work is not primarily academic but explicitly hortatory. It is attempting to mobilize practising managers around a new image of their work identity. It pursues its distinct purpose in a profoundly evangelical manner, one designed to challenge and subvert the 'established church' (now fallen, in Peters's eyes) of what is described as 'traditional' management (Hopfl 1992; Pattison 1997). The key dichotomy is between the ossified 'old' which is in need of urgent 'reinvention' and the 'visionary' new, whose demands must be heeded or disaster will result. The dominant metaphors are 'discontinuity', 'instability', 'fluidity' and 'chaos'. Radical transformation is seen as inevitable and as potentially disturbing, as it is in Lash and Urry's epochal schema, but with an added twist (as befits the difference in purpose and hence narrative style): transformation is ultimately good for everyone, even if not everyone can see that, yet.

The basic narrative informing all of Peters's many works is that organizations and their management are operating in an increasingly chaotic environment. This chaos has the capacity to destroy businesses and managers if left unconfronted. The 'threat', in the form of global competition, is at the gates and threatens to lay waste the promised land which has been betrayed by inflexible, complacent and 'amoral' bureaucracy. If managements and organizations are to survive and flourish in a world turned upside down, they need to alter their modes of conduct completely. For the old order is passing away, the old ways cannot work and there is a need for total transformation and, through that, regeneration. However, salvation is at hand if, and only if, the old ways are abandoned and the prophet's commandments obeyed to the letter and with total commitment – hence the call to develop 'a public and passionate hatred of bureaucracy'. You must receive the spirit whereby you too 'face up to the need for revolution' and 'achieve extraordinary responsiveness' (Peters, 1987, pp. 3–4). If you do this, then the future might just be yours. You, too, will be in tune with ultimate reality and will be able to manipulate the creative/destructive forces of chaos – which are a bottom-line inevitability – to your own advantage. You'll be 'liberated', 'emancipated', and 'free' because you've learnt to 'thrive on chaos'. The alternative, which doesn't bear thinking about, is sure-fire death. So choose life, choose 'maximum businessing'.[1]

Deploying this evangelical strategy, Peters sets up a dynamic of fear, anxiety and discontent amongst his would-be followers. An atmosphere of total, but non-specific threat, is evoked – what could be more threatening and unspecific athan 'chaos'? This threat is then blamed on and used to problematize the authority of the present order – the 'rational' bureaucratic culture (Pattison 1997). Recasting specific circumstances into polarities that construct polemical comparisons out of non-comparable terms is a favoured 'technique of negation' deployed by Peters. He conjures up an aggressively polarized world in which businesses are either conspicuously successful – entrepreneurial organizations thriving on chaos – or total failures – formal, hierarchical bureaucratic dinosaurs. There is nothing in between. Peters then reveals his simple message of salvation which people must follow if they are to avoid annihilation and, more positively, become fully developed human beings able to turn the unavoidable chaos to their own advantage. Damnation/irrelevance is not inevitable, but it will be if you don't become that which you have a duty to be – a 'businessed' person.

As Stephen Pattison (1997, p. 137) has indicated, this constitutes something like Peters's basic 'religious system', within which the underlying metaphor for contemporary managerial reality is that of 'chaos'. This understanding is total and unquestionable, as was, Pattison argues, the Old Testament prophets' understanding of God. As Pattison (1997, p. 137) continues, 'to de-personify the transcendent by getting rid of any overt deity, as Peters does, is not to dispose of its transcendent nature, though it may make it less obvious'. The statement that the world is 'chaotic' is a remarkably religious assertion, one whose veracity cannot be questioned or tested: it can only be accepted or rejected. Acceptance of this basic reality is acceptance of an overarching moral order within which all events, meanings and experiences can be situated and explained. It is the gateway into Peters's unified view of the world. Indeed, Peters acts as the channel or voice for the transcendent chaos, which communicates its essence through him. Like a prophet, he issues a number of commandments, which will guide his followers to organizational and personal salvation. These culminate, as Pattison (1997, p. 138) indicates, in an injunction to intensive and ceaseless effort on the part of every individual member of an organization, no matter what their status or standing.

But this wilful and continuous change and transformation on the part of organizations and persons is not represented as a painful burden or tedious obligation, nor is it to be undertaken simply for instrumental purposes. Above all, it is a means to self-fulfilment and complete development. The wholeness that the bad old bureaucratic past rent asunder is to be recovered, the disenchantment it brought in its wake reversed, through 'maximum businessing', through living life like a business of one. As Peters (1992, p. 755) put it, 'life on the job is looking more like life off the job for a change.

("For a change?" For the first time in a couple of hundred years is more like it.)'

The tone of his commands is direct, didactic and highly moral. Peters is a charismatic leader, in Weber's terms, attempting to organize life 'on the basis of ultimate principles' (Weber 1978, I, p. 467). Indeed, Peters (1987, p. 149) is quite explicit that adopting his epochal worldview is akin to a 'religious conversion'. In this way, the 'management revolutionary' as charismatic religious prophet enthrones himself as moral judiciary. His claim is to unify, through the strategy of 'maximum businessing', that which 'bad old bureaucracy' is held to have set apart as separate spheres of existence: work and leisure, reason and emotion, public and private. For the epochalist prophet, this 'vision' or unified view of the world offers the route to salvation.

As Charles Turner (1992, p. 12), has argued, for instance, epochal accounts such as those offered by Peters and Lash and Urry depend upon 'the extrapolation from one set of predicates to the set of all possible predicates, upon the globalisation of a local phenomenon, in which the one-sidedness of a specific problematic becomes the universality of a general problem'. The more they seek to offer a systematic or 'totalizing' account of the epoch, the more abstract that account becomes: the systematicity promised by the epochal formulation (old/new economy; bureaucracy/enterprise; modern/ postmodern) being brought at the cost of a denial of locatedness and of specificity. In other words, rather than offering an account rooted in an empirical analysis, they deploy instead an abstract hermeneutic whose formulation of the character of 'the epoch' has the necessary effect of drowning out or making invisible the specificity of empirical history. In so doing, they express what Weber (1949, p. 55) termed 'the speculative view of life' and Schmitt (1986, pp. 74–5) the romantic attitude of 'fanciful construction'.

Schmitt's acerbic comment suggests that epochal diagnoses should not be taken seriously. Yet, from the point of view of developments in many contemporary organizational domains, it is Schmitt's perspective which can appear as 'fanciful'. In the life-order of government across the liberal-democratic world, for instance, regimes of many different political hues are home to prestigious exponents of the 'epochal arts'. Epochal theorists such as Anthony Giddens, Geoff Mulgan and Charles Leadbeater, for example, have all been involved, either implicitly or explicitly, with the development of public policy in Britain's New Labour government, and the epochal formulations and designations they or their compatriots are associated with (the third way; connexity; the knowledge-driven economy and so on) can be seen to structure reforms in many areas of governance – not least in the field of public management and 'governance.'[2] This suggests an important point. It is not enough simply to show how empirically 'wrong' epochal analyses might be. Rather, it is important to show what work a particular 'epochalist' discourse might be performing in any given context (as the chapters by Elgaard Jensen and Strannegård and Bergström in this collection indicate). After all, it is clear that much of what was taken for epochal economic change during the 1990s – under the rubric of the old/new economy dualism – has been challenged by the events since the 2000 Nasdaq crash, which helped redefine the new economy as a bubble economy whose dynamics could be perfectly well understood through orthodox economic modelling (Boyer 2000). However, it is also clear that such an account only takes us so far. For one thing, the new economy epochalism had a number of profound effects with which a host of actors – fund managers, policy makers and individual investors, for example – have been left to grapple with over the last few years. Neither these nor a host of other agents find themselves in exactly the same worlds that they inhabited prior to the emergence of the 'new economy' story. That epochalist discourses are constitutive of economic and organizational action implies that such discourses can indeed be performative, even if they are not self-fulfilling prophecies (MacKenzie and Millo 2003). At the very least, we can say that the work that the new economy discourse performed, no matter how one judges its 'empirical' veracity, left a very large number of institutions and persons in significantly 'changed' conditions (Williams 2001).

WORK IDENTITY

If the tyranny of the 'epochal' is a chronic condition in the academic discussion of organizational change in general, then it reaches its apogee in discussions of work identity in particular. Over the last decade or so, a veritable avalanche of epochal analyses devoted to the discussion of 'work identity' have appeared. Many of these – such as Rifkin's *The End of Work* or Sennett's *The Corrosion of Character* – have had a considerable impact not only within academia but also on policy discussions at the highest levels in government and the private sector. Indeed, the idea that work identity is undergoing some profound and irreversible changes has become something of an established 'fact' among a range of commentators, many of whom have had little previous connection to ongoing academic and policy debates about work and organization.[3] Although somewhat different in terms of their style and ethos, critical sociological texts such as Bauman's *Work, Consumerism and the New Poor*, Beck's *The Brave New World of Work* and Sennett's *The Corrosion of Character*, and more upbeat or emancipatory texts such as Peters's *Liberation Management*, Champy's *Re-Engineering Management* or Leadbeater's *Living on Thin Air* share two things. First, an unshakeable belief that work and the identities it offers has changed profoundly. Secondly, they offer their assessment of the changes through the prism of an epochalist analytic. This is evidenced in the dramatic distinctions routinely drawn between past and future work, at both a societal as well as an individual level. Bauman (1998, p. 17), for instance, states that in the past 'work was the main orientation point, in reference to which all other life pursuits could be planned and ordered'. He then proceeds to claim that under present conditions this is no longer the case:

> A steady, durable and continuous, logically coherent and tightly-structured working career is however no longer a widely available option. Only in relatively rare cases can a permanent identity be defined, let alone secured, through the job performed (Bauman, 1998, p. 27)

As with so much of his work, Bauman deploys a template in which the present – taken as a bundle of abstracted attributes and labelled 'postmodern' – is dramatically contrasted with the past – another loose bundle of attributes named 'modern'. For Bauman, work was collectively oriented in the past, individualized in the present; driven by production in the former, by consumption in the latter. This has some crucial implications for identity. In the past workers, however poor, could obtain some meaning, identity and dignity from work, but in a post-modern consumer society (the present) where work loses its centrality, the poor become flawed consumers and identity is contingent and shifting, dependent upon the ability to consume, rather than anchored in a stable production regime. From this analysis is drawn the following conclusion:

> Whatever identity one may contemplate and desire must possess, just like today's labour market, the quality of flexibility. It must be amenable to change at short notice or without notice and be guided by the principle of keeping all options, or at least as many options as possible, open (Bauman 1998, p. 28).

Beck offers a remarkably similar analysis, arguing that the certainties of the past, linked of course to stable patterns of employment and the mythic 'job for life', have 'disappeared'. As a result the ability to derive identity from work is now very precarious, and in contrast to the past, a thoroughly individualized rather than collective enterprise. He states, *au* Bauman, that under these conditions 'normal life stories are breaking up into fragments' (Beck 2000, p. 3). Interestingly, the basic structure of the analysis is almost identical to the dramatic and overblown characterizations of the epoch provided by the managerialists Peters and Champy. While the politics espoused by the sociological epochalists tend to be rather more pessimistic than that of the managerialists, the epochal logic of their arguments, and crucially, many of their substantive claims, are absolutely identical. Now, while a number of the individual claims made by these authors have been subject to convincing critique in recent years, along a wide range of empirical axes (Wajchman and Martin, 2001; see also Chapter 6 by Westenholz, this volume), they have often failed to address adequately the epochalist frame within which such claims about work identity are made. In other words, while individual elements of the discussion of identity might be problematized empirically, the epochalist frame still remains in place. One of the reasons for stressing this point is to distinguish the position outlined in the present volume from a number of recent analyses – and not simply those of our main epochalist protagonists: Bauman, Beck, Peters *et al.* – that have, explicitly or implicitly, viewed changing forms of identity and subjectivity as consequences of wider economic, social and cultural transformations – modernity, postmodernity, the risk society, the network society and so on. These kinds of analyses fail to challenge the epochalist imprimatur precisely because they end up emulating it. They do so by regarding changes in the ways that human beings understand and act upon themselves as the outcome of 'large scale', abstract processes and events – in 'culture', in 'production', in 'consumption', in 'technology' and so on. As Nikolas Rose (1996, p. 129), has argued, for instance, this mentality tells us nothing about the practical ways in which particular forms of identification and subjectivity are constituted or formed. Changing forms of subjectification, he suggests, cannot be established by derivation or interpretation of such abstractions. 'To explicitly or implicitly assume that they can is to presume the continuity of human beings as the subjects of history, essentially equipped with the capacity for endowing meaning' (1996, p. 130). By this he means that the ways in which we give meaning to experience are themselves multiple and styled to suit specific purposes. They are not a reflex capacity that we carry around with us all the time. Rather, they are contingent and relational. Devices of meaning production, for instance – mechanisms such as grids of visualization, vocabularies, norms and techniques of judgement – produce our experience; they do not simply produce experience. These techniques don't come ready made either, out of the ether; rather they have to be invented, refined, stabilized, disseminated and reproduced in a variety of different ways in a number of differing practices – boardrooms, factories, schools, families and so on. As Rose (1996, p. 130) indicates, if we refer to 'identification' or 'subjectification' to 'designate all those heterogeneous processes and practices by means of which human beings come to relate to themselves and others as subjects of a certain type, then subjectification has its own history. And the history of subjectification is more practical, more technical and less unified' than epochalist analyses allow for or appreciate.

Thus, analysing processes of 'subjectification' requires a focus on the relational practices through and in which human beings become 'persons' of a certain sort. This is not the sort of history of the self presumed in accounts such as Beck's, Bauman's or Sennett's, but rather an account of the diversity of languages of 'personhood' that have emerged – character, personality, honour, citizen, individual, human resource, networker – and the norms and techniques of conduct within which they have circulated in legal, organizational and other practices for acting on the conduct of human beings. Thus, we are less concerned here with advancing a simple narrative of the 'self' and its historical changes than with focusing upon the relations, techniques and forms of training and practice through which human beings have acquired certain forms of 'personhood' or 'identity'.

This is a more modest, but perhaps more productive way of exploring the question of 'work identity' than that proposed by epochal sociologies and their managerial counterparts. Rather than simply assuming that the demands of 'organizational flexibility', for instance, create 'individualized' subjects, we should instead analyse the norms and techniques through which particular forms of 'flexibility' are styled in specific contexts and explore the sorts of person they both presuppose and practically make up. We might be surprised by what we find: that flexibilities do not all point in the same direction or presuppose similar human capacities or attributes of their subjects (Westenholz, this volume); that 'bureaucratic norms and techniques' and the persons they constitute might be more supple and agile, and less mechanistic and anachronistic than is commonly assumed (du Gay 2000; Law 2000). Indeed, it might make us see that when the norms and techniques of conduct framing and formatting a particular work identity change, so that the persons they presuppose are thought about and acted towards differently, then we don't simply have the same identity in a different context but rather a new identity. This may, as Ursell, for instance, suggests (Chapter 2, this volume), make us rather more attentive to the practices we jettison when we see how they relate to other persons and things we value. For, if the vocabularies and practices of a given enterprise are not extrinsic to the persons they constitute, then discarding them in favour of other vocabularies and practices might mean risking the loss, for good or ill, of the persons they call into being.

NOTES

1. 'Businessing' represents individuals and groups as 'units of management', and requires that they adopt a certain 'entrepreneurial' form of relationship as a condition of their effectiveness and of the effectiveness of this sort of strategy. As Peters (1994, p. 73) explains, to be businessed is to be given responsibility and to be held accountable for 'running one's own show inside the organization'.
2. Anthony Giddens is an internationally renowned sociologist and, at the time of writing, Director of the London School of Economics. His epochalist political tracts *Beyond Left and Right* (1994) and *The Third Way* (1998), have led him to be labelled as the British 'New'

Labour government's 'intellectual guru'. Geoff Mulgan and Charles Leadbeater came to prominence through their involvement in the 'New Times' project of the influential but now defunct magazine *Marxism Today*. Mulgan went on to help found and then direct the think tank Demos before becoming a political adviser to the New Labour Government in 1997. He is at the time of writing a Senior Civil Servant in the Cabinet Office and Director of the Performance and Innovation and Forward Strategy Units. His characterization of the current 'epoch' is contained in his (1998) *Connexity*. Charles Leadbeater is perhaps best known for his populist epochal tome (1999) *Living on Thin Air*, in which he argues for 'knowledge' as the driving force of contemporary economy and society. The book cover contains an enthusiastic endorsement by the British Prime Minister, Tony Blair, and Leadbeater's influence on New Labour policy formulation can be detected in a number of areas, most notably, perhaps, in The Department of Trade and Industry's (1998) policy document *Our Competitive Future: Building the Knowledge Driven Economy*.
3. One of the interesting side effects of the growing standing of 'epochal analysis' within the fields of organizational analysis has been the manner in which it has altered the identity of the field in terms of the status of its practitioners. By this I mean simply that the most notable and influential tracts on the future of work identity within the social sciences tend to be written by intellectuals with little or no 'track record' in the field of economic sociology or organization studies. This may or may not be a problem for the field, but it is without doubt a noteworthy development.

REFERENCES

Bauman, Z. (1998), *Work, Consumerism and the New Poor*, Milton Keynes: Open University Press.
Bauman, Z. (2000), *Liquid Modernity*, Cambridge: Polity Press.
Beck, U. (2000), *The Brave New World of Work*, Cambridge: Polity Press.
Boyer, R. (2000), 'Is a Finance-led Growth Regime a Viable Alternative to Fordism? A Preliminary Analysis', *Economy & Society*, **29** (1): 111–45.
Callon, M. (1998), 'Introduction: the Embeddedness of Economic Markets in Economics', in M. Callon (ed.), *The Laws of the Markets*, Oxford: Blackwell.
Castells, M. (2000), *The Rise of the Network Society*, 2nd edn, Oxford: Blackwell.
Champy, J. (1995), *Re-engineering Management: The Mandate for New Leadership*, London: Harper Collins.
Department of Trade and Industry (1998), *Our Competitive Future: Building the Knowledge Driven Economy* (Cm 4176), London: HMSO.
DiMaggio, P. (1994), 'Culture and Economy', in N. Smelser and R. Swedberg (eds), *The Handbook of Economic Sociology*, Princeton: Princeton University Press.
Douglas, M. and B. Isherwood, B. (1979), *The World of Goods: Towards an Anthropology of Consumption*, Harmondsworth: Penguin.
Du Gay, P. (2000), *In Praise of Bureaucracy: Weber/Organization/Ethics*, London: Sage.
Du Gay, P. and M. Pryke (eds) (2002), *Cultural Economy: Cultural Analysis and Commercial Life*, London: Sage.
Foucault, M. (1986), 'Nietzsche, Genealogy, History', in P. Rabinow (ed.), *The Foucault Reader*, Harmondsworth: Penguin.
Giddens, A. (1994), *Beyond Left and Right*, Cambridge: Polity Press.
Giddens, A. (1998), *The Third Way*, Cambridge: Polity Press.
Hopfl, H. (1992), 'The Making of the Corporate Acolyte: Some Thoughts on Corporate Leadership and the Reality of Organizational Commitment', *Journal of Management Studies*, **29** (1): 23–34.

Lash, S. and J. Urry (1994), *Economies of Signs and Space*, London: Sage.
Law, J. (1994), *Organizing Modernity*, Oxford: Blackwell.
Law, J. (2000), 'Ladbroke Grove, or How to Think about Failing Systems', http://www.comp.lancs.ac.uk/sociology/papers/law-ladbroke-grove-failing-systems.pdf (accessed 2 April 2004).
Law, J. (2002), 'Economics as Interference', in P. du Gay and M. Pryke (eds), *Cultural Economy*, London: Sage.
Leadbeater, C. (1999), *Living on Thin Air*, Harmondsworth: Penguin.
MacKenzie, D. and Millo, Y. (2003), 'Constructing a market, performing theory: the historical sociology of a financial derivatives exchange', *American Journal of Sociology*, **109**: 107–445.
Mulgan, G. (1998), *Connexity*, London: Vintage.
Osborne, T. (1998), *Aspects of Enlightenment*, London: UCL Press.
Pattison, S. (1997), *The Faith of the Managers*, London: Cassell.
Peters, T. (1987), *Thriving on Chaos*, Basingstoke: Macmillan.
Peters, T. (1992), *Liberation Management*, Basingstoke: Macmillan.
Peters, T. (1994), *The Pursuit of Wow!*, New York: Random House.
Rifkin, J. (1996), *The End of Work: The Decline of the Global Labor Market and the Dawn of the Post-market Era*, New York: Putnam.
Rose, N. (1996), 'Identity, Genealogy, History', in S. Hall and P. du Gay (eds), *Questions of Cultural Identity*, London: Sage, pp. 128–50.
Schmitt, C. (1986), *Political Romanticism*, Cambridge, MA: MIT Press.
Sennett, R. (1998), *The Corrosion of Character: The Personal Consequences of Work in the New Capitalism*, London: Norton.
Turner, C. (1992), *Modernity and Politics in the Work of Max Weber*, London: Routledge.
Wajchman, J. and B. Martin (2001), 'My Company or My Career: Managerial Achievement and Loyalty', *British Journal of Sociology*, **52** (4): 559–79.
Weber, M. (1978), *Economy and Society* (2 vols), Los Angeles: University of California Press.
Williams, K. (2001), 'Business as Usual', *Economy & Society*, **30** (4): 399–411.

Index

account management, advertising industry 19–21
'accumulation' 15, 57, 75–6
acquaintances, view of network as 61–2, 67–72, 74–5
Adie, K. 49
advertising 15, 17
　account management 19–21
　as constituent material practice 18
　historical development of 17–28, 29–30
　media planning 21–4
　research by industry 24–8
Alexanderson, O. 80–81
Alvesson, M. 82
Angell, A. 49, 50
Atkinson, J. 46

Barker's (advertising agency) 21–2
Baudrillard, J. 14
Bauman, Z. 14, 62–3, 154
BBC (British Broadcasting Corporation) 40, 46
Beck, U. 13, 154
belonging, and identity 57–8
Björkman, I. 82
'boundary object' 95
Bourdieu, P. 41–2
Bowker, G.C. 95
Bromley, M. 45
Browne, R. 19, 23, 25
Buckley, S. 36
Burns, T. 40

Calcutt Committee 39
Carlyle, T. 37
Castells, M. 9, 11–13, 15, 34–5, 42, 56, 81
chain, view of network as 60–61, 62, 64–7, 70–72
chaos (Peters) 150–51

club, view of network as a 59–60, 62, 64–70
Cochoy, F. 27–8
commodity-signs 14
communities of practice 57–8
company, as source of identity 127, 130, 131, 136–8, 139, 141
consumption 14–15, 29–30, 148, 154
'cultural intermediaries' 41–2, 44
culturalization of work 147–50
　historical view of 9–17, 28–30
　advertising industry, development of 17–28
Czarniawska, B. 83, 95, 101

Delano, A. 47–8
DiMaggio, P. 149–50

epochal analysis 2–4, 9–17, 79–81, 147–53
　and work identity 153–6
Evers, G.E. 115
Execency, *see* talent agency case study (Execency)

flexible working patterns
　growth of 1–2, 11–12, 13
　and stability 122–3
　see also IT workers case study (identity in the flexible economy)
Foucault, M. 58, 74, 149
fragmentation of society, and identity construction 101–2
Franklin, R. 46
freelance work, *see* graphic designers case study (self-employment and identity); IT workers case study (identity in the flexible economy)

Gay, P. du 16, 34
Giddens, A. 101, 102

159

Index

globalization, effects on journalism 35, 42, 49–50
Gorz, A. 9
graphic designers case study (self-employment and identity) 99–100
  conclusion 119–20
  discourses of other identities 117–19
  'freelance discourse' 105–8, 112–16, 118–19
  future careers, discourses on 111–12
  identity construction at art college 104–8
  'professional community discourse' 108–11, 116–17
  research context/method 102–4
  theoretical perspective 100–102

Habermas, J. 36
hackers 128–9
Hall, S. 123
Halloran, J.D. 44, 47
Hanna, M. 48
Harcup, T. 38
Henderson, H. 21
Henningham, J. 47–8
Himanen, P. 128
homepages 59
Hopkins, C. 24–5
Hower, R. 20

identification (identity construction) 101
identity
  as a 'boundary actor' 95–7
  belonging, and identity 57–8
  company, as source of identity 127, 130, 131, 136–8, 139, 141
  conceptualization of 30, 34–5, 57–8, 73–6
  construction of (theory) 4, 82–3, 100–102, 123–5
  epochal analysis and work identity 153–6
  field identity stories 127–31
  practice identity stories 132–42
  'legitimizing identity' 34, 35, 36–7
  'resistant identity' 34, 35, 37–41
  self-employment, and identity 73, 127–8
  stories, social construction of identity through 123–5

and working life, summary of issues 1–4
'individualization' 11–12, 13, 29, 34–5
'informationalism' 11
Institute of Journalists (IOJ) 37–8
IT workers case study (identity in the flexible economy) 122–5
  'Citizen in the Company' 127, 130, 131, 136–8, 139, 141
  conclusion 142–4
  field identity stories 127–31
  'Free Agent in the Market' 127–8, 130, 131, 134–6, 139, 140–42
  'Open-Source Grassrooter' 128–9, 130, 131, 132–4, 138–40
  practice identity stories 132–42
  'Project Maker in a Professional Community' 129, 130, 131, 139, 141
  research design 125–6

James Walter Thompson (JWT, advertising agency) 20, 21, 24, 25, 26–7
Jenkins, R. 100, 101
Johansson, J. 83–5
Johnson, T. 35, 39
Jones, N. 47
journalism case study (identity formation) 34–6, 50–51
  21st century 41–2
  autonomy and status of journalists 44–9
  institutionalization ('legitimizing identity') 36–7
  mobility, geographical 49–50
  professionalization ('resistant identity') 37–41
  social and cultural role of journalists 43–4
Julier, G. 102, 107

Kant, I. 62, 63
Kelly, K. 79–80

Lash, S. 14, 15, 24, 148–9, 150
Law, J. 16, 59
'legitimizing identity' 34, 35, 36–7
Lyotard, J.-F. 42

Maddocks, J. 20–21
Mansfield, F.J. 38
marketing 21; *see also* advertising
meaning creation 124–5, 155
media planning, advertising industry 21–4
Mitchell, C. 22
Mol, A. 59
'multi-activity society' 13
Murphy, D. 46

Nance, J. 21
National Union of Journalists (NUJ) 37–9
Negus, K. 41
'network society' 42
networking case study (United Spaces) 76
   analytical procedure 63–72
   conceptualizations of identity 57–8, 73–6
   environments 55–6
   'filled space' (Bauman/Kant) 62–3
   forms of networking 59–62
   network-as-a-chain 60–61, 62, 64–7, 70–72
   network-as-a-club 59–60, 62, 64–70
   network-as-acquaintances 61–2, 67–72, 74–5
   reconciliation of different network versions 72–3
   tensions between different network versions 64–72
Nixon, S. 41

One of a Kind, *see* graphic designers case study (self-employment and identity)
organization, and construction of identity 2–3, 82–3, 94–7; *see also* IT workers case study (identity in the flexible economy)
organizational change, and epochal analysis 147–53
Osborne, T. 147, 149

Paine, T. 37
Pattison, S. 151
personal histories, as conceptualization of identity 57, 75

Peters, T. 150–52
Pink, D.H. 73
Piore, M. 46
polarization of work 12, 151
Press Association (PA) 45–6
Press Complaints Commission (PCC) 39–40
Press Council 39
'project identity' 34–5, 49
Pryke, M. 16
Puffelen, F. van 115

Rado, G. 47
Ray, L.15–16
Raymond, C. 19, 23
'reflexive accumulation' 15
Reich, R.B. 42
research, by advertising industry 24–8
'resistant identity' 34, 35, 37–41
Rose, N. 30, 155

Sabel, C. 46
Samson Clark (advertising agency) 23–4
Sayer, A. 16
Schlesinger, P. 44
Schmitt, C. 152
Schumacher, B. 115
'scientific advertising' 24–5
self-employment, and identity 73, 127–8; *see also* graphic designers case study (self-employment and identity); IT workers case study (identity in the flexible economy)
Sell's (advertising agency) 19, 20–21, 22, 23
Sennett, R. 13–14, 57, 75, 122–3
'sense making' 101, 119
Smart, B. 14
Smulders, P.G.W. 115
stability, and flexibility 122–3
Star, S.L. 95
stories, social construction of identity through 123–5
subjectification 58, 155–6
'symbolic analysts' 42

talent agency case study (Execency) 79, 83–5
   agency as a boundary actor 94–7
   clients 90–91

demise of agency 91, 93–4
diagrammatic representation 92
industrial change 87–9
labour market change 85–7
operation of agency 91
'talents' 89–90
Trossmark, P. 80–81
Tulloch, J. 39
Turner, C. 10, 152

United Spaces, *see* networking case study (United Spaces)
Urry, J. 14, 15, 24, 148–9, 150

visibility 74

Wainwright, M. 47
Weber, M. 152
Weick, K. 83, 101, 119, 124
work ethic, demise of 13–14
work identity, and epochal analysis 153–6